DELIVERANCE 101:
A Simple Guide for the Beginner

JOANN WITHERSPOON

Copyright © 2019, JoAnn Witherspoon

All rights reserved. No part of this book may be used or reproduced by any means, graphic, electronic, or mechanical, including photocopying, recording, taping or by any information storage retrieval system without the written permission of the publisher except in the case of brief quotations embodied in critical articles and reviews.

Unless otherwise indicated, all Scripture quotations are taken from the King James Version of the Bible.

All scripture quotations marked AMP are taken from the Holy Bible, Amplified, Copyright © 1954, 1958, 1962, 1964, 1965, 1987, 2015 by the Zondervan (subsidiary of News Corp) and The Lockman Foundation. Used by permission.

All scripture quotations marked NIV are taken from the Holy Bible, New International Version, Copyright © 1973, 1978, 1984 by the International Bible Society. Used by permission.

All scripture quotations marked ASV are taken from the American Standard Version, Copyright © 1901, 1929 by Thomas Nelson & Sons. Used by permission.

All scripture quotations marked NLT are taken from the New Living Translation, Copyright © 1996, 2004, 2015 by Tyndale House Foundation. Used by permission.

All scripture quotations marked RSV are taken from the Revised Standard Version, Copyright © 1946, 1952, 1971 by the Division of Christian Education of the National Council of the Churches of Christ. Used by permission.

All scripture quotations marked TLB are taken from the Holy Bible, The Living Bible Version, Copyright © 1971 by Tyndale House Publishers. Used by permission.

All scripture quotations marked MSG are taken from the Holy Bible, The Message Version, Copyright © 2002 by Eugene H. Peterson. Used by permission.

ISBN-13: 978-1688763777

Edited and formatted by Water2WinePress Publishing House,
a Subsidiary of Ink Well Spoken
www.inkwellspoken.com

DEDICATION

I want to thank my Heavenly Father first for loving me and setting me free from the penalty of death. I thank Him for the awesome gift of the Holy Spirit Who has empowered me and who has led and continues to lead me in this journey of deliverance and healing (emotionally and physically).

*To my beloved grandmother, the late **Rev. Iceola Starling**. She planted and watered the seed of the word in me and God gave the increase. I am the fruit of her labor.*

*To **Apostle Arnetta "Neddie" Salazar**, my sister. She took me by my hand to instruct and encourage me to pursue God with everything I had. She challenged me to discover my purpose and to get busy fulfilling it. Thank you for your love and support when no one else understood nor had the fruit of "longsuffering" to endure with and for me.*

*To my dear mother, **Dorothy Robinson**. You gave me life. Although you may not have understood the reason why, God had a plan. The plan was to use you to bring me forth as a prophet to the nations. I bless and honor you MOTHER.*

*To my sisters **Joan** (my twin) and **Latrice**. My life was never dull! You saw the good, the bad and the ugly and you didn't stop praying for me. You didn't stop believing that one day there would be a change. Indeed it is so!*

*My children, **Armonie, Annjo** and **Adam**. I love you with all my heart and I thank God that He blessed me with you. Truly God gave me the strength and wisdom that I needed to bring you up in the fear and admonition of Him. I could not have done it without Him. His love kept us all!*

*My grandchildren, **Ari, Morgan, Nathan** and **Marcus**, each of you are my delight.*

TABLE OF CONTENTS

DEDICATION	p. iv
ACKNOWLEDGEMENTS	p. vii
INTRODUCTION	p. 1
CHAPTER 1: **WHAT IS DELIVERANCE?**	p. 7
CHAPTER 2: **WHO OR WHAT ARE WE BEING DELIVERED FROM?**	p. 19
CHAPTER 3: **THE MYSTERY OF MARINE DEMONS**	p. 43
CHAPTER 4: **YOUR DELIVERANCE**	p. 63
CHAPTER 5: **THE HOLY SPIRIT**	p. 89
CHAPTER 6: **RESTORATION OF THE FRAGMENTED SOUL**	p. 99
DEFINITIONS	p. 115
BIBLIOGRAPHY	p. 127
ABOUT THE AUTHOR	p. 129

ACKNOWLEDGMENTS

My Spiritual Influences:

Apostle John Eckhart *of Chicago, IL: Your teaching and preaching on the Apostolic and Deliverance ministry catapulted me into my ministry.*

Dr. Paula Price: *Your revelation has been imparted into me through your writings and continues to help me become a better master in my prophetic office.*

Pastor Pat McManus *of Aurora, IL: You recognized the anointing on my life as we had the honor of serving side-by-side one another; establishing the government of the Church and advancement of the Kingdom of God.*

Apostle Larry and Prophet Tiffany Henderson *of Elgin, IL by way of Dayton, OH: Without the two of you, I would not have written this book. You constantly yet gently pushed me to make "Make full proof of my ministry." This book is a small part of me doing just that. You wouldn't let me go and I'm so grateful you didn't!*

To all my dear friends and family who prayed for me and released a prophetic word to help me along this path, thank you!

Blessings to each of you!

INTRODUCTION

"I will not drive them out from before thee in one year; lest the land become desolate, and the beast of the field multiply against thee. By little and little I will drive them out from before thee, until thou be increased, and inherit the land."
Exodus 23:29-30

"And I will give unto thee the keys of the kingdom of heaven: and whatsoever thou shalt bind on earth shall be bound in heaven: and whatsoever thou shalt loose on earth shall be loosed in heaven."
Matthew 16:19

This book is a compilation of teachings I've done over the years as it relates to deliverance. Though there are many books written on the subject of deliverance, I wanted to see a book address it from a straight-forward approach based on a play-by-play narrative directed largely by the holy scriptures. As such, this book is framed in that manner so that the reader is led to revelation gleaned from passages regarding different aspects of deliverance from Genesis to Revelation. The drive to create this manual also stems from the fact that many believers are in the dark regarding the importance of deliverance. The need for deliverance feeds on ignorance (being kept in the dark). In my twenty plus years of ministry, I have encountered far too many believers who have not been provided a scriptural understanding of deliverance; some don't even know that deliverance exists! They don't even know it is their God-given right as children of the Most High to have access to what belongs to them: liberty from demonic oppression in the presence of the Spirit of God (see 2 Corinthians 3:17). This should not be so for deliverance is the Children's Bread!:

> **deliverance[1]**: n. rescue from bondage or danger
>
> **deliverance[2]** (from the Greek word *aphesis*): n. freedom, liberty, remission; forgiveness; a release from bondage
>
> **deliver[1]**: vb. to bring or transport to the proper place or recipient; distribute; to surrender (something or someone) to another; hand over; to secure (something promised or desired) as for a candidate or political party; to set free, as from misery, peril, or evil
>
> **deliver[2]** (from the Hebrew word *natsal*): vb. to snatch away, whether in a good or bad sense; to defend, escape, preserve, recover, rescue; to tear oneself away

deliver[3] (from the Hebrew word *palat*): vb. to carry away safe; to slip out

deliver[4] (from the Hebrew word *padah*): vb. to sever; to release; to redeem

"And, behold, a woman of Canaan came out of the same coasts, and cried unto him, saying, Have mercy on me, O Lord, thou Son of David; my daughter is grievously vexed with a devil... But he answered and said, I am not sent but unto the lost sheep of the house of Israel. Then came she and worshipped him, saying, Lord, help me. But he answered and said, It is not meet to take the children's bread, and to cast it to dogs. And she said, Truth, Lord: yet the dogs eat of the crumbs which fall from their masters' table. Then Jesus answered and said unto her, O woman, great is thy faith: be it unto thee even as thou wilt. And her daughter was made whole from that very hour." **Matthew 15:22-28**

>**devil** (from the Greek word *daimon*): n. an inferior deity (as in a god or goddess); an evil spirit; demon
>
>**vex** (from the Greek word *ochleo*): vb. to mob or torment
>
>**mob**: n. a group of persons bent on riotous living
>
>**riotous**: adj. participating in a riot

In this passage of scripture, we see that a Canaanite woman is in need of deliverance as her daughter has been vexed with a devil. There have been many false teachings on deliverance. One such teaching states that only those outside of the Christian faith (as the Canaanite woman in this passage of scripture was outside of the Hebrew faith) need deliverance. Yet if you pay attention to this scripture, Jesus stated to the woman that the children's bread is to be delivered to the lost sheep of the house of Israel *first* before it is extended to anyone else! This implies that even the chosen/elect are in need of being freed from demonic oppression. This contradicts the accepted principle that once a person gets saved, they are immediately delivered. While this is true in part, there is more.

The more is this: We are comprised of a spirit and a soul. Why else would the word of God be described as being sharper than a two-edged sword capable of dividing between the soul and spirit (see Hebrews 4:12)? Accepting Jesus as the Christ brings complete salvation to immediately redeem our spirits which are then made to sit in Christ in heavenly places (see Ephesians 2:6) – but what of our souls? They remain with our earthly bodies and are meant to go through a lifetime process known as sanctification. Simply put, sanctification is the continuous yielding of one's life, passions and purpose to the power of God. This simple yet important distinction has not been clearly explained to new converts or to people who continue to struggle with whatever sin issue that's keeping their minds clouded and their souls impure.

Those who have heard of deliverance but have convinced their piously biased selves that it is unnecessary often immediately reject it because it goes against their religious and/or traditional beliefs. Still others, as unfortunate as this is, have fallen into the use of man-made rituals to rid themselves of the flesh's deadly influences upon the soul – passed down from generation to generation as they unknowingly erect strongholds continuously fortified through non-Biblical and false doctrine. We must be careful to avoid these pitfalls as the word of God says:

> "Howbeit in vain do they worship me, teaching for doctrines the commandments of men. For laying aside the commandment of God, ye hold the tradition of men, as the washing of pots and cups: and many other such like things ye do. And he said unto them, Full well ye reject the commandment of God, that ye may keep your own tradition." **Mark 7:8-9**
>
> > **doctrine** (from the Greek word *didache*): n. that which is taught; instruction

While the latter have become entangled in pride, there are many believers at the other end of the spectrum who struggle with sin, guilt and condemnation as they desperately attempt to believe God for their promised freedom without knowing how to access it practically. After years of such vain attempts, they are left with the belief that freedom is beyond their reach as they sink into bouts of hopelessness and defeat; plagued and tortured by mounting questions lingering within:

> 'If I am saved, why do I continue to wrestle with the same thing over and over again?'
>
> 'Why can't I change?'
>
> 'When will my change come?'
>
> 'Why do I have a hard time letting go?'

Or, better yet...
> 'Why does God continue to let this happen to me when I'm doing everything I can to change?!!'

If you've ever struggled with any of these questions, beloved, do not fret! The word of God is quick and powerful!:

> "For the word of God is quick, and powerful, and sharper than any twoedged sword, piercing even to the dividing asunder of soul and spirit, and of the joints and marrow, and is a discerner of the thoughts and intents of the heart."
> **Hebrews 4:12**

> "For it is God which worketh in you both to will and to do of his good pleasure." **Philippians 2:13**

Beloved, I promise you this: I will make every attempt to keep this simple. You, the reader, will know that deliverance IS your daily bread right as a child of the Most High God! Hopefully, as you begin to have your mind renewed and faith restored concerning this important aspect of your Christian life, you can begin your journey towards freedom. A freedom that can only truly be sought through the deliverance Christ gave His life for us to experience through righteousness, peace and joy in the Holy Ghost! Blessings!

CHAPTER 1:
WHAT IS DELIVERANCE?

Before we go "another further," can we address the elephant in the room for a moment? Rather, can we address *The Exorcist* in the room? Though it can be dramatic (depending on the level of generational darkness a given individual is shrouded in), the vast majority of times I've participated in deliverance sessions have NOT been to the level of this FICTITIOUS movie! Yes, we are dealing with demons (unclean spirits), but even THEY must obey the name of Jesus as it comes out of YOUR mouth with authority and assurance!:

> "And there was in their synagogue a man with an unclean spirit; and he cried out, Saying, Let us alone; what have we to do with thee, thou Jesus of Nazareth? art thou come to destroy us? I know thee who thou art, the Holy One of God. And Jesus rebuked him, saying, Hold thy peace, and come out of him. And when the unclean spirit had torn him, and cried with a loud voice, he came out of him. And they were all amazed, insomuch that they questioned among themselves, saying, What thing is this? what new doctrine is this? for with authority commandeth he even the unclean spirits, and they do obey him." **Mark 1:23-27**

> "And the seventy returned again with joy, saying, Lord, even the devils are subject unto us through thy name. And he said unto them, I beheld Satan as lightning fall from heaven. Behold, I give unto you power to tread on serpents and scorpions, and over all the power of the enemy: and nothing shall by any means hurt you. Notwithstanding in this rejoice not, that the spirits are subject unto you; but rather rejoice, because your names are written in heaven." **Luke 10:17-20**

> **tread**: vb. to trample; to hit as if by a single

blow, to smite, to strike; to walk on, over; to press beneath the feet; to subdue harshly or cruelly, crush (see Genesis 3: 14-15)

serpent: n. metaphorically, a serpent is referred to as an artful, malicious person: one who is skillful in accomplishing a purpose, especially with cunning or craft; the malice, the desire to harm others or see others suffer is compared to the venom of a serpent (see Psalm 58:4, 140:3)

scorpion: n. metaphorically, a skeptic, one who doubts, question or disagrees with piercing opposition

"Verily, verily, I say unto you, He that believeth on me, the works that I do shall he do also; and greater works than these shall he do; because I go unto my Father." **John 14:12**

believe: vb. to accept as true or real; to have firm faith in; to have faith, confidence, or trust

belief: n. mental acceptance of and the conviction in the truth, actuality, or validity of something

In order to live this life victoriously while "doing greater works than these," one must desire and know how to be set free from the things that bind him/her. We are told in Matthew 16:19 that Peter was given the keys of the kingdom of heaven. The problem with that is that Peter is dead! If he had been the only person provided with such keys, how can the potential of the church be unlocked if only one man possessed it?!! In truth, the statement Jesus makes to Peter is one that He has made to all who believe on His name. You and I also have the ability to use these keys such that whatever we bind/loose on earth shall be bound/loosed in heaven! THIS IS THE ESSENCE OF DELIVERANCE!

If we think of what a key does, it locks and unlocks. Understanding this concept, binding and loosing correlates to locking and unlocking. There are many things that can be locked and unlocked in the realm of heaven and earth:

- treasure or valuable possessions (both spiritual and earthly)
- secrets (both heavenly and worldly)
- people (mental and physical imprisonment)

Deliverance deals with the latter. The LORD God desires His people to worship Him in spirit and in truth... but the truth of the matter is this: though where the Spirit of the Lord, there ought to be liberty amongst His believers – there is not. As God's peculiar treasure (see 1 Peter 2:9), He desires us to be unlocked, unbound and unfettered!:

> "(For he had commanded the unclean spirit to come out of the man. For oftentimes it had caught him: and he was kept bound with chains and in fetters; and he brake the bands, and was driven of the devil into the wilderness.)" **Luke 8:29**

> "And when Jesus saw her, he called her to him, and said unto her, Woman, thou art loosed from thine infirmity." **Luke 13:12**

While the woman in Luke 13 was bound to an infirmity which Jesus healed her of; many of us are bound in spiritual and mental chains which He desires to break us out of as He did in Luke 8.
That said, let's break open this concept a little further.

BINDING AND LOOSING

"And I will give unto thee the keys of the kingdom of heaven, and whatsoever thou shalt bind on earth shall be bound in heaven: and whatsoever thou shalt loose on earth shall be loosed in heaven."
Matthew 16:19

> **bind** (from the Greek word *deo*): vb. to fasten or tie as with chains, when Satan is bound he is made inoperable.
>
> **loose** (from the Greek word *lyo*): vb. to loose any person or thing tied or fastened; to loose one bound; to set free; to discharge from prison; to free from bondage or disease (one held by Satan) by restoration to health; loosing is setting the captive free

For the purposes of this book, binding refers to demonic activity in a person's life. Binding and loosing are interrelated in that loosing a person who has been bound by the forces of darkness also binds the demonic activity. As such, when Satan's work is bound, the victim is loosed. He is the strong man spoken of whom we are shown needs to be bound in Luke 11:

> "When a strong man armed keepeth his palace, his goods are in peace: But when a stronger than he shall come upon him, and overcome him, he taketh from him all his armour wherein he trusted, and divideth his spoils." **verses 21-22**

You have been made stronger than the strong man in Christ! The power to bind and loose has been given to the church by Jesus Christ to continue the work He began on Calvary. The devil's regime which we war against is stubborn. Though the eviction notice rang clear from Jesus' resurrection, they are still active in the lives of humanity – relying on the curse of the law to stay amongst our ranks through loopholes and darkness. Though this redemptive work has defeated our adversary, the devil's regime is still very much active on the earth which is why WE are charged to make His enemies His footstool (see Hebrews 10:13) on earth as it already stands in heaven.

This is the meaning of "whatsoever we shall bind on earth shall be bound in heaven" and "Thy kingdom come. Thy will be done in earth, as it is in heaven" in Matthew 16:19 and Matthew 6:10, respectively. NONE are bound and tortured in heaven that are called to be the bride of Christ (the Church) – and earth is to reflect what is in heaven.

Likewise, there are things in heaven (demonic activity) that have already been bound, outlawed and/or forbidden; so whatever activities from the kingdom of darkness that have been locked up in heaven but are still free to move about the countries of the earth should not be so. Basically, whatever is bound or loosed by the believer is done on the basis that it has already been done in heaven.

HAUNTED HOUSE:
GETTING GOD'S HOUSE IN ORDER

Redeemed from a "condemned" status, the body of the believer is meant to "house" God's Holy Spirit as His temple (see I Corinthians 3:16). As such, each believer becomes a lively stone in a "spiritual house" which is not made of hands:

> "What? know ye not that your body is the temple of the Holy Ghost which is in you, which ye have of God, and ye are not your own? For ye are bought with a price: therefore glorify God in your body, and in your spirit, which are God's."
> **I Corinthians 6:19-20**

> "Ye also, as lively stones, are built up a spiritual house, an holy priesthood, to offer up spiritual sacrifices, acceptable to God by Jesus Christ."
> **I Peter 2:5**

> "We heard him say, I will destroy this temple that is made with hands, and within three days I will build another made without hands." **Mark 14:58**

This temple exists in heaven even as the shadow of its substance was first created in the Old Testament before being ransacked and destroyed the last time in 70 AD. Though the physical temple was destroyed, the spiritual temple was already completed and holy – nothing missing, nothing broken. Yet the balance between what exists in heaven versus what exists in earth is out of order; and God is all about (getting His house in) order. In heaven, the beings dwelling in the temple are of pure light (including believers washed by the blood of Jesus).

> "Forasmuch as ye know that ye were not redeemed with corruptible things, as silver and gold, from your vain conversation received by tradition from your fathers; But with the precious blood of Christ, as of a lamb without blemish and without spot:" **I Peter 1:18-19**

> > **corrupt**: vb. to ruin, to decay, to spoil by any process; defile, destroy; to be marked by immorality and perversion; to ruin morally; to change the original form of a thing/person

> **defile**: vb. to make foul or unclean; to pollute, taint; debase; to make impure for ceremonial use; to make filthy or dirty

Unlike the beings of pure light in heaven, the earthly, soulish beings, though... us?!! Not so much! We are riddled with darkness. The soul of the average believer is plagued by uncleanliness which is why it must be swept and garnished:

> "When the unclean spirit is gone out of a man, he walketh through dry places, seeking rest, and findeth none. Then he saith, I will return into my house from whence I came out; and when he is come, he findeth it empty, **swept, and garnished**. Then goeth he, and taketh with himself seven other spirits more wicked than himself, and they enter in and dwell there: and the last state of that man is worse than the first. Even so shall it be also unto this wicked generation."
> **Matthew 12:43-45 (emphasis added)**

Unclean spirits have made themselves at home in our house (the how and why is addressed in CHAPTER 3)! They are the proverbial thieves in the temple! Though the Holy Spirit indwells in us legally, unclean spirits do so, as well (albeit it illegal). Think of them as squatters.

Pigs in the Parlor, an excellent book on deliverance written by Frank and Ida Mae Hammond, describes these demons further as trespassers: ones who unlawfully and stealthily encroach the territory of another.

> **trespass:** vb. an unlawful act causing injury to the person, property or rights of another, committed with force or violence; it is an overstepping of boundaries and assuming possession of another's property.

> **stealth**: n. secret, the act or practice of stealing
>
> **encroach**: vb. to advance beyond proper, established, or usual limits; to trespass upon property, domain, or rights of another, especially; by gradual advances; it also means to creep gradually and often
>
> **squatter**: n. a person who settles on land or occupies property without title, right, or payment of rent

Think of this from a farmer's perspective for a moment. If you've ever grown a garden, no matter how small, you know that it will eventually attract mongrels looking for a free meal!:

> "Take us the foxes, the little foxes that spoil the vine: for our vineyards are in blossom."
> **Song of Solomon 2:15**

Now let's consider a landlord's perspective. Once a trespasser/squatter is discovered, landlords typically tend to deal with them rather aggressively, yes? If not, trespassers will continue their unlawful practices until confronted and challenged based on the legal rights of both the tenants and the landlord. As tenants and landlords, it's of utmost important we know our legal rights as believers. No demons have access to the title of anybody redeemed by the blood of Jesus!

Yet and still, evil spirits will put up every possible roadblock to keep people from knowing their rights which is why keeping us in the dark is such an integral part of their strategy! They know that knowledge of this truth will set us free and kick them out!

And they've gotten good at hiding in the dark. The longer

they remain undetected, the safer they'll remain in their place of residence as it's passed on from parent to child in unending cycles we've come to know as generational curses. I don't know how much experience you have with this, but that sounds like a timeshare! I know... this is scary stuff, right?!! But to God be the glory for He has given us a way out through salvation *and* deliverance!

Deliverance, by way of the discerning of spirits (the seventh gift of the Holy Spirit as found in I Corinthians 12:10), affords us a strategy of our own to counteract this darkness. The only way to destroy a cover of darkness is to bring it into the light. Discerning the unclean spirit(s) operating within a person brings the enemy out of hiding by way of exposure. Not forgetting that we are in spiritual warfare when speaking of deliverance, once an enemy is discovered, it is to be destroyed. In his book *Let Us Alone*, John Eckhart tells us that this fear of being destroyed is an extremely strong motivation for our adversary to avoid being located as he stays in hiding:

> "But these five kings fled, and hid themselves in a cave at Makkedah. And it was told Joshua, saying, The five kings are found hid in a cave at Makkedah... Then said Joshua, Open the mouth of the cave, and bring out those five kings unto me out of the cave... And afterward Joshua smote them, and slew them, and hanged them on five trees: and they were hanging upon the trees until the evening." **Joshua 10:16, 17, 22, 26**

These kings had much to fear! They had heard of the hand of the LORD moving on those that opposed the children of Israel – and that same hand is upon us! Only now, the work of dispossessing larger than life enemies in the physical realm accomplished in the Old Testament must be done in the spiritual realm:

"And having spoiled principalities and powers, he made a shew of them openly, triumphing over them in it." **Colossians 2:15**

"In this way, God disarmed the spiritual rulers and authorities. He shamed them publicly by his victory over them on the cross."
Colossians 2:15 NLT

The enemy fears the coming of the LORD through the work of our hands and the mighty name of Jesus! That said, when the word of the Lord says that we are to work out our own salvation with fear and trembling, it is not the same type of fear (see Philippians 2:12)! We should honor deliverance for what it is. In other words, respect the process by:

1) Not being afraid of or discrediting it
2) Acknowledging its existence and relevance for today's believer
3) Acknowledging the need for it in YOUR life as a part of the sanctification process that begins after salvation

CHAPTER 2:
WHO OR WHAT ARE WE BEING DELIVERED FROM?

DELIVERANCE FROM SATAN'S POWER

God's kingdom is one of light. Therefore, it goes to reason that His adversary's opposing kingdom is one of darkness. Though we were all born into sin (and thus born into darkness), those who are called back to God's purpose and righteousness are meant to be translated out of the darkness and into the marvelous light (see 1 Peter 2:9); ushered in by Jesus as the light of the world. This process is what sanctification is all about and continues long after salvation is accepted. We are to be drawn out of the power of darkness through a lifestyle of transparency. Darkness not only being a literal word but figurative concerning our ignorance of the spiritual kingdom around us which houses very real curses and very real blessings which are operating against and for us, respectively. We are to no longer live in the shadows of our sins but in the confessed freedom purchased by the Son of God and maintained in the Holy Ghost!

> **sin**: n. transgression of divine law; any act regarded as a transgression: especially a willful or deliberate violation of some religious or moral principle; any regrettable action or behavior; great fault or offense
>
>> **transgress**: vb. to violate a law, command or moral code; to pass over or go beyond a limit or boundary imposed by a law or command; to violate: especially the will of God

To be clear, the devil and his demons rule the darkness. There is darkness in this world and the Lord tells us not to love this world for to love this world is to love the devil and his demons.

> "For we wrestle not against flesh and blood, but

against principalities, against powers, against the rulers of the darkness of this world, against spiritual wickedness in high places." **Ephesians 6:12**

"Love not the world, neither the things that are in the world. If any man love the world, the love of the Father is not in him. For all that is in the world, the lust of the flesh, and the lust of the eyes, and the pride of life, is not of the Father, but is of the world." **I John 2:15-16**

>   **lust**:   n.   desire (for what is forbidden), craving, longing

"To open their eyes, and to turn them from darkness to light, and from the power of Satan unto God, that they may receive forgiveness of sins, and inheritance among them which are sanctified by faith that is in me." **Acts 26:18**

"Who hath delivered us from the power of darkness, and hath translated us into the kingdom of his dear Son." **Colossians 1:13**

Do you know how much power the sun generates? Neither do I! But I do know this – light is more powerful than darkness. There is no competition between the two. I've heard of solar power but I've never heard of anyone harnessing power from the dark in terms of energy consumption, preservation and generation. While the earth is powered by the sun, the saints of God are powered by the SON! Check out Luke 10:19:

>   "Behold, I give unto you power* to tread on serpents and scorpions, and over all the power** of the enemy: and nothing shall by any means hurt you." (emphasis added)

SPECIAL NOTE: there are two powers at work in this scripture:

power* (from the Greek word *exousia*): n. in the sense of ability, lawful authority

> **authority** (from the Greek word *exousaizo*): vb. to have power, use power, exercise authority upon; ability or strength with which one is endued, which either possesses or exercises; to command such that one must be submitted to by others and obeyed; to enforce laws, exact obedience, command, determine, or judge

> **power**** (from the Greek word *dynamis*): n. strength power, ability, power residing within a thing by virtue of its nature or which a person or thing exerts and puts forth; power whether by virtue of one's own ability and resources, or of state of mind, or through favorable circumstances, or by permission of law or custom; miraculous power: ability, might; (worker of) power, strength, mighty works; the word "dynamite" stems from this word

This authority is what we have over the strength of the enemy... but where does such authority come from? It comes directly from Jesus' (KING of kings!) victory over sin and death which we inherit through salvation. It is the power set obtained through baptism in the Holy Ghost.

"But ye shall receive power, after that the Holy Ghost is come upon you:" **Acts1:8a**

"And these signs shall follow them that believe; In my name shall they cast out devils;"
Mark 16:17a-b

WHY ARE WE IN NEED OF DELIVERANCE?

We need deliverance because we've adopted the philosophies (the use of reason in understanding such things as the nature of the real world, our existence, the use and limits of knowledge, and the principles of moral judgment) of man. We fluctuate between different doctrines or beliefs all while constantly being deceived and defrauded (see Ephesians 4:14).

The carnal mind is enmity against God. Carnality is a combination of fleshly lust and sensual desires. What does that entail, you ask? Whatever sounded, looked and felt good which we did to walk in our flesh instead of according to the Holy Spirit (see II Corinthians 5:21) and God's Will. Moreover, because we were born into a world of sin and shaped by the iniquity within it, we are more inclined to operate in the power of darkness. When we didn't know God, we were without Christ and without hope as we lived according to the ways of the world (see Ephesians 2:12).

"For though we walk in the flesh, we do not war after the flesh: (For the weapons of our warfare are not carnal, but mighty through God to the pulling down of strong holds;) Casting down imaginations, and every high thing that exalteth itself against the knowledge of God, and bringing into captivity every thought to the obedience of Christ;" **II Corinthians 10:5**

"They are darkened in their understanding and separated from the life of God because of the ignorance that is in them due to the hardening of their hearts." **Ephesians 4:18 NIV**

"Because that, when they (man) knew God, they

glorified him not as God, neither were thankful; but became vain in their imaginations, and their foolish heart was darkened. Professing themselves to be wise, they became fools," **Romans 1:21-22 (amplification added)**

WHAT IS SPIRITUAL BLINDNESS?

Spiritual blindness is the condition that an individual has when they are unable to see God or understand His message. As a result, the individual is unable to lay hold of, seize, take possession of or comprehend his/her spiritual inheritance: the invisible Kingdom of God.

"The light shines in the darkness, but the darkness comprehended it not." **John 1:5**

> **comprehend** (from the Greek word *katalambano*): vb. to lay hold of (so as to make one's own); to obtain, attain to, to take into one's self; to seize upon, take possession of (especially of evil: overtaking one, of the last day overtaking the wicked with destruction, of a demon about to torment one; especially of Christ: by His holy power and influence laying hold of the human mind and will, in order to prompt and govern it); to detect, catch; to lay hold of with the mind; to understand, perceive, learn

"Hell and destruction are never full; so the eyes of man are never satisfied." **Proverbs 27:20**
"Now the natural man receiveth not the things of the Spirit of God: for they are foolishness unto him; and he cannot know them, because they are spiritually judged." **I Corinthians 2:14 ASV**

"The god of this age has blinded the minds of unbelievers (those that do not trust God), so that they cannot see the light of the gospel of the glory of Christ, who is the image of God." **II Corinthians 4:4 NIV**

"The enemy does not want you to believe anything God has said. He (the devil) was a murderer from the beginning, and abode not in the truth,
because there is no truth in him. When he speaketh a lie, he speaketh of his own: for he is a liar, and the father of it." **John 8:44 (amplification added)**

"Again, therefore Jesus spake unto them, saying, I am the light of the world: he that followeth me shall not walk in the darkness, but shall have the light of life." **John 8:12 ASV**

"For you were once darkness, but now you are light in the Lord. Live as children of light:" **Ephesians 5:8**

"[Jesus] told him, "Go wash yourself in the pool of Siloam" (Siloam means 'sent'). So the man went and washed and came back seeing!... 'How then were your eyes opened?' they asked. He replied, 'The man they call Jesus made some mud and put it on my eyes. He told me to go to Siloam and wash. So I went and washed, and then I could see.'... A second time they summoned the man who had been blind. 'Give glory to God by telling the truth,' they said. 'We know this man is a sinner.' He replied, 'Whether he is a sinner or not, I don't know. One thing I do know. I was blind but now I see!' " **John 9:7, 10-11, 24-25 NIV (amplification added)**

"Immediately, something like scales fell from Saul's eyes, and he could see again. He got up and was baptized." **Acts 9:18 NIV**

Question: How do you see Jesus?

WHO OR WHAT CAN BRING YOU INTO SPIRITUAL BLINDNESS?

SIN ITSELF

Any unconfessed sin that has not been repented of gives demons legal right to remain in your soul. It's as simple as that.

"I acknowledged my sin unto thee, and mine iniquity have I not hid. I said, I will confess my transgressions unto the LORD; and thou forgavest the iniquity of my sin. Selah." **Psalm 32:5**

"Search me, O God, and know my heart: try me, and know my thoughts: And see if there be any wicked way in me, and lead me in the way everlasting." **Psalm 139:23-24**

"For all that is in the world, the lust of the flesh, and the lust of the eyes, and the pride of life, is not of the Father, but is of the world." **I John 2:16**

"He that committed sin is of the devil; for the devil sinneth from the beginning." **I John 3:8a-b**

"Let no man say when he is tempted, I am tempted of God; for God cannot be tempted with evil, neither tempteth he any man: But every man is tempted, when he is drawn away of his own lust, and enticed. Then when lust hath conceived, it bringeth forth sin, when it is finished (full grown), bringeth forth death." **James 1:13-15 (amplification added)**

"Whosoever committeth sin is the bondservant of sin." **John 8:34c**

"Know ye not, that to whom ye yield yourselves servants to obey his servants ye are to whom ye obey whether of sin unto death, or of obedience unto righteousness?" **Romans 6:16**

> 'Servants of sin are at the beck and command of sin; they give up themselves to the service of it with delight and diligence, and are perfect drudges to it: this is a very unhappy situation; their service is very unreasonable; and they are rendered incapable of serving God, for no man can serve two masters; they are hereby brought into the drudgery of the devil; into a state of bondage.' – John Gill

FALSE GODS/IDOLS

While idols were primarily inanimate objects fashioned to look like anything found in heaven or earth for men to worship in the Old Testament, nowadays, idols and false gods are more akin to mental strongholds. Specifically, they amount to anything that you build or lift up in reverence as high as (if not higher than) the Word, Will or Personage of God.

"Howbeit then when ye knew not God, ye did service unto them which by nature are no gods." **Galatians 4:8**

"Before you Gentiles knew God; you were slaves to so-called gods that do not even exist." **Galatians 4:8 NLT**
"But now that you know God – or rather are known by God – how is it that you are turning back to those weak and miserable forces? Do you wish to be enslaved by them all over again?" **Galatians 4:9 NIV**

"Ye know that ye were Gentiles, carried away unto these dumb idols, even as ye were led." **I Corinthians 12:2**

SEDUCERS

Seducers entice us with consistent resistance to our better judgment and moral stance against sin. They are patient and conniving. They convince us with the desires of our hearts through the weakness of our flesh until we come into agreement (covenant) with longstanding temptations. The enemy temps us when we are vulnerable (under physical and emotional stress) as well through our strengths where we are susceptible to pride. Know this: seducers, tempters and temptresses do not discriminate. They even attempted to tempt the Christ, so you *know* they're going to try you! You're no less susceptible to them than Jesus was, yet you have the same power He possesses to overcome (see Matthew 4:1-11)!

> **seduce**: vb. to lead astray, as from duty; to corrupt; to lead or draw away, as from principles, faith, or allegiance; to win over; to attract or entice

> **entice**: vb. to beguile by something (as an action or speech) that tends to flatter or coax; to allure, to bait (as to catch by or with bait)

"While they promise them liberty, they themselves are slaves of corruption; for by whom a person is overcome, by him also he is brought into bondage. For if, after they have escaped the pollutions of the world through the knowledge of the Lord and Savior Jesus Christ, they are again entangled in them and overcome, the latter end is worse for them than the beginning. For it would have been better for them not to have known the way of righteousness, than having known it, to turn from the holy commandment delivered to them. But it has happened to them according to the true proverb: 'A dog returns to his own vomit,' and, '"a sow, having washed, to her wallowing in the mire.'" **II Peter 2:19-22 NKJV**

"The Lord knoweth how to deliver the godly out of temptations, and to reserve the unjust unto the day of judgment to be punished." **II Peter 2:9**

"No temptation has overtaken you that is not common to man. God is faithful, and he will not let you be tempted beyond your strength, but with the temptation will also provide the way of escape, that you may be able to endure it." **I Corinthians 10:13 RSV**

APOSTASY

Though one's salvation cannot be lost if you truly believed in your heart and confessed "Jesus is Lord" with your mouth, there is a consequence to rejecting the faith. Turning away from the Christian faith for any reason is like leaving the back door open to your once-secured home. Quite simply, it leaves you vulnerable to break-ins. Even simpler, the best instruction one can receive to avoid apostasy is to listen AND act when Jesus speaks!

> **apostasy**: n. the abandonment or renunciation of a religious or political belief

> **apostate**: n. one who abandons or renounces a religious or political belief

"See that you do not refuse Him who speaks. For if they did not escape who refused Him who spoke on earth, much more shall we not escape if we turn away from Him who speaks from heaven," **Hebrews 12:25 NKJV**

"Demas hath forsaken me, having loved this present world," **II Timothy 4:10a-b**

"Love not the world, neither the things that are in the world. If any man loves the world, the love of the Father is not in him. For all that is in the world, the lust of the flesh, and the lust of the eyes, and the pride of life, is not of the Father, but is of the world and the world passeth away, and the lust thereof: but he that doeth the will of God abideth for ever." **I John 2:15-17**

"Not giving up meeting together, as some are in the habit of doing, but encouraging one another – and all the more as you see the Day approaching. If we deliberately keep on sinning after we have received the knowledge of the truth, no sacrifice for sins is left, but only a fearful expectation of judgment and of raging fire that will consume the enemies of God. Anyone who rejected the law of Moses died without mercy on the testimony of two or three witnesses. How much more severely do you think someone deserves to be punished who has trampled the Son of God underfoot, who has treated as an unholy thing the blood of the covenant that sanctified them, and who has insulted the Spirit of grace? For we know him who said, 'It is mine to avenge; I will repay,' and again, 'The Lord will judge his people.' It is a dreadful thing to fall into the hands of the living God… But we do not belong to those who shrink back and are destroyed, but to those who have faith and are saved." **Hebrews 10:25-31, 39 NIV**

> **deliberate**: adj. done with or marked by full consciousness of the nature and effects of one's actions; intentional; voluntary
>
> **habit**: n. an act repeated so often that it becomes involuntary; there is no new decision of the mind each time the act is performed

"And even as they did not like to retain God in their knowledge, God gave them over to a reprobate mind, to

do those things which are not convenient... Who knowing the judgment of God, that they which commit such things are worthy of death, not only do the same, but have pleasure in them that do them."
Romans 1:28, 32

>**reprobate** (from the Greek word *adokimos*): adj. not standing the test; that which does not prove itself such as it ought; unfit for, unproved

STRONGHOLDS

stronghold¹ (physical): n. an enclosure that is fortified with thick stonewalls; a fortress built with walls and defenses to provide protection against the enemy, usually built on a hill so attackers had to climb up to reach the fortress

>**fortify**: vb. to strengthen and secure (a place, such as a town) by forts; to give physical strength, courage, or endurance to

stronghold² (spiritual) n. speculations and imaginations

stronghold³ (from the Greek word *ochyroma*): n. reasonings, thoughts, and imaginations that precede and determine our conduct; the arguments and reasoning's by which a disputant endeavors to fortify his opinion and defend it against his opponent.
>**disputant**: n. one that is engaged in a dispute; arguer

Strongholds are mental, willful and emotional fortifications set up by unclean spirits that block or "quench" the Holy Spirit from operating in our lives. Strongholds can start off as the forceful opinions, stubborn arguments, and excuses of the mind that justify our stances which oppose the truth of God. Once they're set up, though the spirit of a believer is secured in Christ, the soul's ability to freely move about and operate in God's Kingdom on earth becomes limited. Think of it as an unholy military occupation in territory that's meant to be liberated by the indwelling of the Holy Spirit.

Once these reasons and arguments become justifications, we hold on to them to lock ourselves in; but in fact, they lock us in. Many times, the best way to spot a stronghold is by how much a person will "dig in" on a particular stance no matter how rationally or lovingly you convince them that they are in error. Strongholds become weapons that the enemy can use to enslave us or fragment our souls. They are the perfect nesting ground for the enemy to torment us with things that happened in our past.

> **torment**: vb. to afflict with great bodily or mental suffering or pain; to weary or annoy excessively; to throw into commotion; stir up; to disturb

As we remember those things that were done to us or things we used to do, the enemy's mission is to keep us hostage or to have us continually looking back: using regret, shame, betrayal, abuse (physical, emotional, mental or sexual), rejection, abandonment or even a lack of affirmation, safety and security.

When a person is bound in a stronghold, they find false protection, security and familiarity in said stronghold. This is a trap – much like drug addicts in a crack (or "trap") house. Instead of safety, one becomes a captive prisoner (see Joshua 6:1b). Truth cannot be fully received when in such a place as it cannot be heard through the thick walls of such.

Over time, the sins we struggle with create strongholds the more familiar such sins become to us. Such familiarity breeds a type of comfort that becomes a protection which we will defend at all costs. Such defensiveness is a sign of Stockholm Syndrome – a mental condition where prisoners become so dependent on their captors that they will go as far as picking up weapons to defend their abductors when rescuers attempt to free them. These walls are often relied upon to ensure that no one (even loved ones) can come in to hurt us or dislodge the root behind such sin/strongholds: unclean spirits. Though we want someone to come in and love us, they are often driven away by these spirits since love, which can usher in freedom, covers a multitude of sins (see I Peter 4:8). This creates a state of double-mindedness in the believer.

You can be shown love, kindness, exhortation and compassion. You can be warned, logically reasoned with, cautioned against failing to do what is required by God or even threatened – yet you will remain in this stronghold. Liberators (including Christ the Redeemer!) who try to enter are deemed to be intrusive invaders and may be run off (with the exception of Jesus) as they're dealing with their own strongholds favoring self-preservation in a fight that will surely end with one person not going out the same way they came in – with battle scars, to boot! That's why strongholds are often defensive standoffs. They usually have a spiritual army of squatter-soldiers perched on the walls of your mind ready to take aim and fire to protect their illegal right to be housed within you! They may have even been extracted before but they're quite prone to return… with reinforcements!:

"When the unclean spirit is gone out of a man, he walketh through dry places, seeking rest; and finding none, he saith, I will return unto my house whence I came out. And when he cometh, he findeth it swept and garnished. Then goeth he, and taketh to him seven other spirits more wicked than himself; and they enter in, and dwell there: and the last state of that man is worse than the first." **Luke 11:24-26**

Every stronghold has a general principality (king or ruler) governing the unseen forces which must be discerned and dealt with appropriately. You can't destroy the stronghold and leave the principality untouched! If you leave the general to his own devices, all he's going to do is move his war crimes to another place and set up operation all over again. First, find the stronghold, discern the principality and then go after both of them.

These generals and unclean spiritual armies are in allegiance to Satan; but the last thing he wants is for us to recognize him which is why you won't be able to see him if you are spiritual blind to his tactics. In II Corinthians 2:11b, God's Word says:

"for we are not ignorant of his devices."

Whether actively (violent, aggressive, hostile) or passively (non-violent, non-aggressive or even cordial) resistant, strongholds come in many different shapes and sizes – custom fit for every individual based on family lineage and personal vices. Either way, Satan has a fiery arsenal which is thrown in the form of words. These fiery darts can come as three different types of projectiles:

1. fiery stones
2. fiery arrows
3. fiery javelins

Each of these reflects fiery imagery illustrating that these satanic soldiers are determined to protect the strongholds they've managed to create in each of us. They will maim, kill, and destroy anyone that tries to take their fortress, but don't fret! We've been given proper weaponry to defend and go on the offense with, as well!:

> "For we wrestle not against flesh and blood, but against principalities, against powers, against rulers of the darkness of this world, against spiritual wickedness in high places. Wherefore take unto you the whole armour of God, that ye may be able to withstand in the evil day, and having done all, to stand. Stand therefore, having your loins girt about with truth, and having on the breastplate of righteousness; And your feet shod with the preparation of the gospel of peace; **Above all, taking the shield of faith, wherewith ye shall be able to quench all the fiery darts of the wicked.** And take the helmet of salvation, and the sword of the Spirit, which is the word of God:" **Ephesians 6:12-17 (emphasis added)**

More important than our own spiritual munitions, we have a general that sits far above the highest fortification Who, though He lived life as a man, was never compromised! Jesus had no hidden lies, impure motives, corrupted lineage or selfish attitudes/motives that Satan could use as an open door to influence His soul:

> "For the prince of this world cometh, and hath nothing in me." **John 14:30b-c**

HALLELUJAH!!

What Are Strongholds Composed of within the Mind?

Strongholds can consist of the following:

1. A collection of thoughts that are lies against what God has revealed about Himself.
   a. Recall that the devil is a liar and the father of them (see John 8:44)
   b. Recall that the devil speaks great words against the Most High (see Daniel 7:25)

2. Habit structures of thoughts in the area of our soul that can influence the negative thought patterns of our life.

3. Habitual lies that we've embraced and built up by a foundation of lies and half-truths. A fortress of thought that influences the way we respond to the truth about God's character within us.

4. A safe haven where demons hide and are protected.

5. High places that exalt themselves above the knowledge of God (see II Corinthians 10:5)

6. Wrong motivations and attitudes that protect and defend a person's walk in the flesh.

7. Hidden places within our soul we don't recognize or identify as sin as we take on the attitude: "That's just the way I have always been."

8. Blockages that keep a person from repenting and seeking the Lord.

9. A core of the soul so afflicted that it sends twisted thoughts and emotions throughout the mind.

Stronghold Objectives

These are some of the purposes of strongholds:

1. To produce negative thoughts within us in order to block us from giving or receiving love.

2. To restrict our knowledge of God.

3. To give us tunnel vision so we don't see wrong from right.

4. To shape our value system and how we value and treat others.

5. To distort our spiritual priorities in life and cause us to do things we don't want to do.

6. To hinder us from receiving and walking in truth

7. To make straight thinking difficult by guarding our weak spots with false feelings and emotions.

8. To send negative messages to our souls.

9. To cause us to draw negative conclusions as to how to relate to and fellowship with people.

"For though we walk in the flesh, we do not war after the flesh: for the weapons of our warfare are not carnal (of the flesh), but mighty through God to the pulling down of strongholds; Casting down imaginations, and every high thing that exalteth itself against the knowledge of God, and bringing into captivity every thought to the obedience of Christ; and having a readiness to revenge all disobedience, when your obedience is fulfilled." **II Corinthians 10:3-6**
"That which is born of the flesh is flesh and that which is born of the Spirit is spirit." **John 3:6**

BAD HABITS

When left alone for long enough, habits, both good and

bad, take on lives of their own. For this reason, habits are created by a series of choices that give birth to the habit. Subconsciously, habits operate with their own automated reactions maintained to the point that they drive the voices each of us hear which talks to and directs us all the time. This may sound devious but not all habits are demonic by nature! Demonic influences function best by perverting and usurping our (super)natural functionality.

As the saying goes from Stephen Covey's book *The Seven Habits of Highly Effective People*:

> 'Sow a thought, reap an action; sow an action reap a habit; sow a habit, reap a character; sow a character, reap a destiny.'

That being the case, the question becomes:

> How should we develop our minds to lean towards more constructive versus destructive habits?

That's a great question – I'm glad you asked!:

> "Trust in the LORD with all thine heart; and lean not unto thine own understanding. In all thy ways acknowledge him, and he shall direct thy paths." **Proverbs 3:5-6**

> "And be not conformed to this world: but be ye transformed by the renewing of your mind, that ye may prove what is that good, and acceptable, and perfect will of God." **Romans 12:2**

We are called "not to conform any longer to the pattern of this world." Habitual patterns of pride, rebellion, stubbornness, arrogance, covetousness, selfishness, jealousy, envy, strife and hatred evolve into lifestyles of sin which are harder to break than a one-time transgression. What you put into your mind determines what comes out in your words/actions as well as the strength of strongholds mentioned in the latter section.

Mental fortresses become strongholds as our thoughts continue to dwell upon feelings of fear, insecurity, offense, unbelief, doubt, lust, control, striving, unrest, bitterness, resentment, criticisms, unforgiveness or habitual sin. As such, fleshly responses automatically come up out of habit as our thought patterns begin to take on a structure that ultimately isolates us from the Spirit of God.

Until these habitual lies are uprooted, torn down, overthrown, and destroyed, it will be difficult to walk in the Spirit and manifest the presence of Christ when situations warranting His power present themselves. Only when the Holy Spirit renews, re-educates and re-directs our mind are we truly transformed:

> "For they that are after the flesh do mind the things of the flesh; but they that are after the Spirit the things of the Spirit." **Romans 8:5**

"Do mind" means to exercise, entertain or be mentally disposed in a certain direction. So, this passage of scripture is urging us to set our souls' affection on being like or of the same kind of mindset as the Spirit rather than thinking according to our flesh. When we think according to our flesh, we tend to make a habit out of assumptions rather than truth-seeking according to the Word of God. Assumptions leave room for interpretation; and if we don't allow the Word of God to interpret itself prompted by the leading of the Holy Spirit (instead of preferring to lean on our own understanding), we... will... err.

Presumptuous erring are sins we commit when we presume our conduct is acceptable to God when, in fact, it offends Him:

> "Who can understand his errors? cleanse thou me from secret faults. Keep back thy servant also from presumptuous sins; let them not have dominion over me: then shall I be upright, and I shall be innocent from the great transgression." **Psalm 19:12, 13**

In truth, the only thing we should assume to presume is the mind of Christ (see I Corinthians 2:14-16). This is a real possibility and expectation for the believer who has been grafted into the Body of Christ with Jesus as the Head! In this type of corporal environment, the Holy Spirit indwells within us as we dwell in Jesus (see John 15:4-7)! Through the Holy Spirit, we cannot only begin to know God's thoughts but conversations with Him where He answers us as much as we speak to Him! After all, if your brain sends a signal to a member of your body but can't get a signal sent back (or vice versa), the body is considered to be out of alignment, isn't it?!! The synaptic habit of two-way communication must be kept in-tact.

> "Let this mind be in you, which was also is Christ Jesus." **Philippians 2:5**

> "But I see a different law in my members, warring against the law of my mind, and bringing me into captivity to the law of sin which is in my members." **Romans 7:23**

Essentially, to have the mind renewed in its thinking is to not be conformed to religion but to be conformed to the image of Christ. New mind, new habits, new nature...

Question. Are you making it a habit to spend enough time with Christ so as to have His mind in you?

"Take my yoke (coupling) upon you, and learn of me; for I am meek and lowly in heart: and ye shall find rest for your souls." **Matthew 11:29 (amplification added)**

"For I have given you an example that you should do as I have done to you." **John 13:15**

"He that saith he abideth in him ought himself also so to walk, even as he walked." **I John 2:6**

"Finally brethren, whatsoever things are true (correct, factual, real), whatsoever things that are honest (authentic), whatsoever things are just (fair), whatsoever things that are pure (unpolluted, clean, wholesome) whatsoever things are lovely (lovable), whatsoever things that are of a good report; if there be any virtue, and if there be any praise, think on these things."
Philippians 4:8 (amplification added)

CHAPTER 3:
THE MYSTERY OF MARINE DEMONS

What Are Marine Demons and Where Did They Come From?

According to Genesis' account, God gathered the waters together in seas and set boundaries for them before commanding the dry land to appear.

> "In the beginning God created the heaven and the earth. And the earth was without form, and void; and darkness was upon the face of the deep. And the Spirit of God was brooding upon the face of the waters." **Genesis 1:1-2**

> "And God said, Let the waters under the heaven be gathered together unto one place, and let the dry land appear: and it was so. And God called the dry land Earth; and the gathering of the waters Seas: and God saw that it was good." **Genesis 1:9-10**

> "The earth is the LORD'S, and the fulness thereof; the world, and they that dwell therein. For he hath founded it upon the seas, and established it upon the floods." **Psalm 24:1-2**

To this day, the depths of our oceans are so vast that the majority of them remain a mystery to mankind. In fact, it's been said that they're even less explored than the surface of the moon!

Since ancient times, it's been understood that earth's vast bodies of water have been dominated by dark forces; yet this is not how God intended them to be. Teeming with life (even the fowl of the air were called out of it in Genesis 1:20), there are rivers of God that bring blessings and healing as water itself is a symbol of life. Just as there are natural rivers in the earth, there are spiritual rivers, as well:

> "And he shewed me a pure river of water of life, clear as crystal, proceeding out of the throne of God and of the Lamb." **Revelation 22:1**

> "He that believeth on me, as the scripture hath said, out of his belly shall flow rivers of living water." **John 7:38**

Such rivers bring blessings of healing, deliverance and joy. Though water itself is not evil, much like everything God has created, its purpose can be corrupted by powers that oppose God. God's power in creation is used to restrict these rebellious spirits and make earth inhabitable for and maintained by mankind. But when we don't maintain the earth with the God-given power we've been endowed with, malevolent powers are waiting in the wings to overflow God's majestic seas with demonic rivers which cause death and destruction to flow into the world. These powers are called "marine demons."

Marine demons draw their strength from waters (natural and spiritual). When waters are dried up their powers are broken. Marine demons are the offspring of fallen angels that were cast down from heaven to earth (see Rev. 12:9). These fallen angels closely connected to the catastrophic flood of the Old Testament which is where the water affiliation stems. You know the story but there's an important piece that often goes overlooked:

> "And it came to pass, when men began to multiply on the face of the earth, and daughters were born unto them, **That the sons of God saw the daughters of men that they [were] fair; and they took them wives of all which they chose... There were GIANTS in the earth in those days; and also after that, when the sons of God came in unto the daughters of men, and they bare [children] to them, the same [became] mighty men which [were] of old, men of renown.** And

GOD saw that the wickedness of man [was] great in the earth, and [that] every imagination of the thoughts of his heart [was] only evil continually. And it repented the LORD that he had made man on the earth, and it grieved him at his heart."
Genesis 6:1-2,4-6 emphasis added

Though we know that this passage of scripture is the prelude to the flood, we typically gloss over the fact that there were giants in the land as a result of the "sons of God... took them wives of all which they chose." Many have incorrectly assumed that these sons of God were merely human beings but Jude 1:6 provides important clarification:

> "And the angels which kept not their first estate, but left their own habitation, he hath reserved in everlasting chains under darkness unto the judgment of the great day."

> **habitation** (from the Greek word *oiketerion*): n. a dwelling place; of the body as a dwelling place for the spirit

Angels, being spiritual beings of heaven and made by God, are children of the Lord just as much as we are. As sons go, these particular angels didn't stray far from the typical model of sons as they rebelled, left their Father's house (heaven) AND had sex with women of earth! Their offspring (viewed as an abomination by God) were "giants in the earth in those days":

> **giant** (from the Hebrew word *nephiyl*): n. giants, the Nephilim (derivative of the Hebrew word *naphal*); Anakim of Philistia and Emims of Moab (see Deuteronomy 2:10-11)

> **naphal**: vb. to fall, lie down, be cast down, fail

This makes sense when you think about it because the giants' angelic parents have historically come to be known as "The Fallen" or "fallen angels." Genesis 6:4 states that not only were the giants in the earth in the days of the flood but also after that – which explains Goliath and his brothers roaming the planet with six fingers and toes on each hand and foot, respectively (see 2 Samuel 21:20).

God charged these fallen angels with folly and punished them by locking them up in hell and making sure they had a front row seat of the destruction of their illegal offspring.

> "Behold, he put no trust in his servants; and his angels he charged with folly:" **Job 4:18**
>
>> **folly**: n. criminally or tragically foolish actions or conduct; evil, wickedness; lewd behavior

The wickedness of man was influenced and driven by these giants as they ravaged the land. Thus, the worldwide flood was God's way of dealing with this infestation on planet earth. The flood disembodied the spirits of the giants which had no place to go since they neither originated in heaven or earth: hiding out in places that felt most comfortable for them: human beings (being part earth, part spirit). While King David successfully waged many war campaigns to cast out the remaining physical giants of the land, the apostolic work of casting out their disembodied spirits was passed on to the son of David and His Bride: King Jesus and the Church!
This sheds new light on Luke 11:24:

> "When the unclean spirit is gone out of a man, he walketh through dry places, seeking rest; and finding none, he saith, I will return unto my house whence I came out."

This proper context is highlighted by the fact that this verse makes a point to stress that an unclean spirit (demon) will go through "dry places" but, upon finding no rest, will return to the person (house) it was cast out of from the beginning. These demons, reborn in earthly waters, operate from under the waters: oceans, seas, lakes, and rivers. They can affect the land when men, consciously or unconsciously, invite them through pacts and unholy acts. After all, Satan and his demons have no power unless it's been given to them by people's rebellion against God.

What Is Their Assignment?

The assignment of marine demons is to bring souls into the kingdom of darkness; making men subject to Satan. The spirits are proud and rebellious as they seduce and motivate people to sin and engage in acts of rebellion against God themselves. They lend strength and support to spiritual wickedness in high places (see Ephesians 6:12). Their mission is to steal, kill, and destroy (see John 10:10). A marine demon (operating as an unclean spirit) occupies or influences a human body to animate and manipulate. It wants a body of its own.

How Can We Identify Marine Demons?

We identify marine demons through spiritual discernment, their character or nature and the works of the flesh (see I Corinthians 12:10, Luke 6:43-44 and Galatians 5:19-21, respectively). While we can recognize unclean spirits operating on land, it can be more difficult to see their influence as they're operating from the water, as there are multitudes of spirits connected to the water which run as deep as the oceans themselves.

These spirits of the marine kingdom are identified in the scriptures as follows:

- Leviathan   Job 41
- Rahab   Joshua 2:9-10
- The Dragon   Isaiah 51:9
- Baal and Dagon   1 Samuel 5:1-5

Leviathan (from the Hebrew word *livyathan*): n. sea monster, dragon

Baal: n. Canaanite god of storms, rivers and water; some text uses Hadad, a god of thunderstorms: also known as the weather god of Syria-Palestine.

Dagon: n. Philistine deity of fertility represented with the face and hands of a man and the tail of a fish (the name itself meaning "fish")

Following this precedent, a marine demon can also be seen as a sea serpent, snake, fish, octopus or squid. They are strong and can go undetected for years as they affect people on land.

The spirits represent a wide range of issues affecting everyday aspects of our lives: lust, sexual sin and debauchery, abuse (physical, mental, emotional, spiritual, sexual and child), witchcraft, perversion, murder, death, pride, rebellion, destruction, and greed. It is interesting to note that they afflict our lives the most in the manner that they first opposed God's Kingdom – through rebellion and sexual perversion (having left their habitation and slept with the women of earth).

debauchery: n. extreme indulgence in bodily pleasures and especially sexual pleasures: behavior involving sex, drugs, alcohol, etc. that is often considered immoral

witchcraft (**witch** stemming from the Indo-European word *weik* used for both the words religion and magic): n. from an old English term *wicce-craft*, referring to the art or skill of using supernatural forces to bend the world (or another person) to one's will; a religion (any system of beliefs, practices, and ethical values) that worships Satan and his demonic forces in order to receive magic power to influence and control the will of others; such practices work primarily through disobedience, which opens the door for intimidation, manipulation and domination

Uncovering how marine demons operate is a matter of Biblical record... once you know what you're looking for with the right context:

" And when he was entered into a ship, his disciples followed him. And, behold, there arose a **great tempest in the sea**, insomuch that the ship was **covered with the waves**: but he was asleep. And his disciples came to him, and awoke him, saying, Lord, save us: we perish. And he saith unto them, Why are ye fearful, O ye of little faith? Then he arose, and **rebuked the winds and the sea**; and there was a great calm. But the men marvelled, saying, What manner of man is this, that even **the winds and the sea** obey him! And when he was come to the other side into the country of the Gergesenes, there met him **two possessed with devils, coming out of the**

> **tombs, exceeding fierce**, so that no man might pass by that way. And, behold, they cried out, saying, What have we to do with thee, Jesus, thou Son of God? art thou come hither to torment us before the time? And there was a good way off from them an herd of many swine feeding. So **the devils** besought him, saying, If thou cast us out, suffer us to go away into the herd of swine. And he said unto them, Go. And when they were come out, they went into the herd of swine: and, behold, the whole herd of swine ran violently down a steep place **into the sea, and perished in the waters.**" **Matthew 8:23-32 (emphasis added; see also Mark 4:35-5:41, Luke 8:22-25)**

While the unclean spirits in this story were tormenting and occupying the body of the man living in the tombs, their activity was first observed in the waters. In fact, Jesus permitted them to return to the waters at the end of the tale once he had cast them out of the man (who was His main concern). Why? They both knew (Jesus and the demons) that God's enemies were already living on borrowed time now that Jesus was walking the planet!:

> "Therefore rejoice, ye heavens, and ye that dwell in them. Woe to the inhabiters of the earth and of the sea! for the devil is come down unto you, having great wrath, because he knoweth that he hath but a short time." **Revelation 12:12**

> **SPECAL NOTE:** It is the swine that perished in the water, not the demons. Remember, water is a symbol of life. If the unclean spirits had been cast out and not permitted to go into swine, they would have been forced to walk in dry (waterless) places,

seeking rest and finding none (**see Matthew 12:43 and Luke 11:24**). Where there is no water, the power of the demons is broken. The marine demons thrive in water. There they have strength: spiritually and physically. This is why they must be cast out of their human hosts: who, much like the earth, are 75% water.

Knowing About Marine Demons: What's the Point?

Knowing about marine demons is important just as it is important in knowing about any enemy or opponent that one faces. After all, how can we effectively fight our enemy if we don't know how he operates? That's like entering into a boxing ring to fight a challenger we can't see! The more we know about marine demons, the less they can take advantage of us. The more we know about marine demons, the less likely we are to be destroyed by them. The Bible makes it clear that our enemy is a strong man. We would do well to know just how strong he is; but not for the purposes of fearing him – for the purposes of casting him out and taking his spoils!:

> "Or else how can one enter into a strong man's house, and spoil his goods, except he first bind the strong man? And then he will spoil his house." **Matthew 12:29**

> "No man can enter into a strong man's house, and spoil his goods, except he will first bind the strong man; and then he will spoil his house." **Mark 3:27**

Though we're dealing with a strong man, do not fear – we are stronger in Christ!:

> "When a strong man armed keepeth his palace,

his goods are in peace: But when a stronger than he shall come upon him, and overcome him, he taketh from him all his armour wherein he trusted, and divideth his spoils. " **Luke 1:21-22**

"I can do all things through Christ which strengtheneth me." **Philippians 4:13**

Know the strongman, bind him and divide the spoil! I can't say this enough - you can't fight offensively if you don't know who the strongman is and how he keeps his house!

Satan's Kingdom

Satan is known by several names – each signifying his oppressive influence over our world:

"Satan" (from the Hebrew word *satan*): n. adversary, one who withstands

> "And he said unto them, I beheld Satan as lightning fall from heaven." **Luke 10:18**

"Lucifer" (from the Hebrew word *heylel*) n. light-bearer; shining one, morning star

> "How art thou fallen from heaven, O Lucifer, son of the morning! [how] art thou cut down to the ground, which didst weaken the nations!" **Isaiah 14:12**

"the great dragon/that old serpent, the devil":

> "And the great dragon was cast out, that old serpent, called the Devil, and Satan, which deceiveth the whole world: he was cast out

into the earth, and his angels were cast out with him." **Revelation 12:9**

"the god of this world":

> "In whom the god of this world hath blinded the minds of them which believe not, lest the light of the glorious gospel of Christ, who is the image of God, should shine unto them." **II Corinthians 4:4**

"the prince of this world":

> "Hereafter I will not talk much with you: for the prince of this world cometh, and hath nothing in me." **John 14:30**

"the prince of the power of the air":

> "Wherein in time past ye walked according to the course of this world, according to the prince of the power of the air, the spirit that now worketh in the children of disobedience:" **Ephesians 2:2**

Within Satan's kingdom are his messengers of various ranks. With Satan as their king, this demonic network resists separation and joins themselves tightly together by land, water and air to wage war on and lay hold of their victims: us.

> "For we wrestle not against flesh and blood, but against principalities, against powers, against the rulers of the darkness of this world, against spiritual wickedness in high places."
> **Ephesians 6:12**

A Biblical example of how they lay hold of their victims tightly is the use of Leviathan and his scales:

> "His scales are his pride, shut up together as with a close seal. One is so near to another that no air can come between them. They are joined one to another; they stick together, that they cannot be sundered. These demons operate in and through pride of all kind." **Job 41:15-17**

What are the scales of the Leviathan? Though, we will address them several times over throughout this book, this is by no means a complete list:

- rejection*
- rebellion
- lust
- disappointment
- hurt
- insecurity
- shame
- fear
- self-righteousness
- religious spirits
- anger
- violence
- strife
- contention
- quarreling
- bitterness
- wrath
- envy
- jealousy
- discouragement

> "But now ye put off all of these: anger, wrath, malice, blasphemy, filthy communication out of your mouth." **Colossians 3:8**

> ***SPECIAL NOTE**: Rejection from the womb: The sad reality and wicked strategy of the devil is that seeds of rejection and abandonment can be sown in as early as the womb - when one or both parents neither wanted the pregnancy nor the unborn child. Since the amniotic sac is 98% water, this particular unclean spirit can enter in and gain strength through the water in the amniotic fluid that surrounds the unborn baby.

What's in a Name?

Once you know the name (listed as scales in the previous section) of the demon operating in someone, you can call it out by said name. This name can be an emotion such as anger or even a diagnosed condition such as arthritis. Remember, they've gone undetected and hidden because they've not been called out by name.

Since unclean spirits tend to gather in groupings (forming strongholds), calling them out by name is a way to begin dismantling the group one entity at a time; almost like unraveling a ball of string one strand at a time or peeling an onion. Take the film *Gladiator*, for example. There's a scene where Maximus (the protagonist of the story who was once a Roman general before being sold into slavery), is in the Roman Coliseum with other slaves. Realizing that they had a better chance of survival if they stuck together, he directed the other combatants to remain in close ranks – no matter what came out at them from the gates. There were some who ended up leaving the core group as they attempted to defend themselves in fear. While they were promptly cut down, those that stayed together lived to fight another day.

In like manner, we're able to pick demons off one-by-one by calling them out at the gate by their names! Speaking their name, through discernment of the Holy Spirit and at the command of the name of Jesus, gives us authority over every name that is named in the earth (see Ephesians 1:21)! This is the essence of spiritual authority and power which every believer possesses! Have you ever heard the expression: "Don't bring a knife to a gun fight"? We cannot win in spiritual warfare battling with natural strength. The natural man cannot receive the things of the Spirit of God (which are spiritually discerned), let alone expel the spirit of the devil (see I Corinthians 2:14, Romans 8:5-8).
    expel: vb. to force or drive out; to discharge from or as if from a receptacle

SPECIAL NOTE: Since "spirit" and "breath" originate from the same Greek word *pneuma*, the general reactions that one may experience when expelling a demon are breath-associated. As the person administering deliverance, you should encourage the person receiving this ministry not to suppress yawning, sighing, groaning, coughing, sobbing, screaming or roaring. These are all manifestations that the unclean spirits are emerging. Make way for these demons to come out. Keep the exits clear (mouth, nostrils and eyes). The person who is experiencing these expulsions should not start praying or speaking in tongues as this can be a barrier to keep demons within them.

The natural man/carnal man is dependent upon the physical senses because his spiritual apparatus is out of commission due to being dead in trespass and sin. This is why, though we walk in the flesh, we do not war in the flesh; for the weapons of our warfare are not carnal but mighty through God to the pulling down of strongholds (see 2 Corinthians 10:3-4)! Any hope we have to live freely and spiritually must be secured by depending on the power of the Holy Spirit – not fleshly logic or might (see Romans 7:14-25). We are exhorted to put off the former manner of thinking (carnal) from our old life (which is corrupt) as we are renewed in the spirit of our minds (see Ephesians 4:22-23).

How Are Marine Demons Cast Out?

Certain principles outlined in this book will mirror one another as we learn to address strongholds for the marine demons operating behind them. Due to this, the recurring themes you may read regarding how to dislodge a particular stronghold or unclean spirit only reinforce the importance of the actions. If you've ever worked out, you know that repetition is the best way to develop muscle growth; and, as it relates to the purpose and practice of deliverance, it's important that we build up good muscle memory. That said, the following scriptures are grouped in a list of practical exercises that are necessary for casting out marine demons:

1. Forgive

deliverance (from the Greek word *aphesis*): n. freedom, liberty, remission; **forgiveness**; a release from bondage

> "Whose soever sins ye remit, they are remitted unto them; and whose soever sins ye retain, they are retained." **John 20:23**

> "Then came Peter to him, and said, Lord, how oft shall my brother sin against me, and I forgive him? till seven times? Jesus saith unto him, I say not unto thee, Until seven times: but, Until seventy times seven." **Matthew 18:21-22**

> "And when ye stand praying, forgive, if ye have ought against any: that your Father also which is in heaven may forgive you your trespasses. But if ye do not forgive, neither will your Father which is in heaven forgive your trespasses."
> **Mark 11:25-26**

2. Use the Word of God

"Wherefore take unto you the whole armour of God, that ye may be able to withstand in the evil day, and having done all, to stand… And take the helmet of salvation, and the sword of the Spirit, which is the word of God:" **Ephesian 6:13,17**

"For the word of God is quick, and powerful, and sharper than any twoedged sword, piercing even to the dividing asunder of soul and spirit, and of the joints and marrow, and is a discerner of the thoughts and intents of the heart." **Hebrews 4:12**

3. Use the Keys of the Kingdom

"And I will give unto thee the keys of the kingdom of heaven: and whatsoever thou shalt bind on earth shall be bound in heaven: and whatsoever thou shalt loose on earth shall be loosed in heaven." **Matthew 16:19**

4. Fast and Pray:

"And one of the multitude answered and said, Master, I have brought unto thee my son, which hath a dumb spirit; And wheresoever he taketh him, he teareth him: and he foameth, and gnasheth with his teeth, and pineth away: and I spake to thy disciples that they should cast him out; and they could not… When Jesus saw that the people came running together, he rebuked the foul spirit, saying unto him, Thou dumb and deaf spirit, I charge thee, come out of him, and enter no more into him. And the spirit cried, and rent him sore, and came out of him: and he was as one dead; insomuch that many said, He is dead. But Jesus took him by the hand, and lifted him up; and he arose. And when he was come into the house, his disciples asked him privately, Why could not we cast him out? And he said unto them, this kind can come forth by nothing, but by prayer and fasting." **Mark 9:17-18, 25-29**

"Is not this the fast that I have chosen? to loose the bands of wickedness, to undo the heavy burdens, and to let the oppressed go free, and that ye break every yoke?" **Isaiah 58:6**

5. Be Obedient to God

"(For the weapons of our warfare are not carnal, but mighty through God to the pulling down of strong holds;) Casting down imaginations, and every high thing that exalteth itself against the knowledge of God, and bringing into captivity every thought to the obedience of Christ; And having in a readiness to revenge all disobedience, when your obedience is fulfilled."
II Corinthians 10:4-6

6. Operate in God's Perfect Timing with Patience

"Moreover the LORD thy God will send the hornet among them, until they that are left, and hide themselves from thee, be destroyed. Thou shalt not be affrighted at them: for the LORD thy God is among you, a mighty God and terrible. And the LORD thy God will put out those nations before thee by little and little: thou mayest not consume them at once, lest the beasts of the field increase upon thee. But the LORD thy God shall deliver

them unto thee, and shall destroy them with a mighty destruction, until they be destroyed."
Deuteronomy 7:20-23

"I will not drive them out from before thee in one year; lest the land become desolate and the beast of the field multiply against thee. By little and little I will drive them out from before thee, until thou be increased, and inherit the land."
Exodus 23:29-30

> **desolation**: n. a state of devastation waste or barrenness

> **desolate**: adj. deprived or destitute of inhabitants, deserted; solitary, lonely; forsaken or abandoned

CHAPTER 4:
YOUR DELIVERANCE

> "He that hath no rule over his own spirit is like a city that is broken down, and without walls."
> **Proverbs 25:28**

So, here's the million-dollar question: Do you need deliverance? Are you a broken-down city without walls? Odds are, you do and you are to some degree. Don't despair – you are not alone! Though I've written this book to be a simple guide for deliverance, I am by no means a subject matter expert. Many others have written books that are definitive and well-documented works regarding the work of this particular ministry. As such, I'm going to return to a pair of my go-to authors on deliverance: Frank and Ida Hammond.

In the sixth chapter of their book *Pigs in the Parlor*, the Hammonds provide an excellent outline which systematically addresses whether or not you need deliverance. The following is a direct reference to this chapter which speaks to seven areas of a Christian's life that foster telltale signs of the need for deliverance. The section title of the third chapter in this book is derived from their sixth chapter title: Seven Ways to Determine the Need for Deliverance.

DISCERNING THE NEED FOR DELIVERANCE

The presence and nature of evil spirits manifesting in our lives can be recognized through two methods:

> **discern(ment)**: vb. to separate, make a distinction (recognize or noting of difference); (see 1 Corinthians 12:10)

> **detect(ion)**: vb. to observe (as it relates to deliverance – to observe what spirits are doing to/through a person)

Not all demonic manifestations are over the top and boisterous. Every deliverance session does not mirror a scene from one of a dozen or so exorcism movies you may have watched or heard about in the past. I have gone head-to-head with a strong spirit of witchcraft that has tossed its occupant out of a chair as it mocked my efforts for up to an hour but I've NEVER had split pea soup projectile-vomited on me nor have I witnessed it in real life! Manifestations differ due either to the varying degrees of personalities demons occupy or the level of said occupation (stronghold). Some are talkative or boastful while others are quiet and secretive. Some respond instantly to being identified and commanded to leave while others resist with a greater degree of stubbornness. Some will manifest and be cast out with no visible manifestations (see Acts 16:16-18); while others can be violent and uproarious (see Luke 9:37-39). Do not fret, though! Remember – you have been made stronger than the strong man in Christ!

While my goal in writing this book is to bring awareness, it is NOT meant to create paranoia and accusation amongst God's people! Not every person who has an outburst of anger or sudden fright is under the influence of an anger or fear demon; but if these emotions become obsessive or habitual, there could be a demon at work. And when there's one... there's bound to be others. Demons tend to operate in groups with one being the primary head. This is done to vex a person in a layered attack which makes it harder to unravel the stronghold being built. Think of an onion. This head demon is often the door-opener and has entry points as far back as our childhood. If left undetected, it will hold the door open for a succession of other demons to follow.

While this is by no means an exhaustive list, we can learn

today to detect evil spirits by simply observing and properly attributing what they are doing to a person through the following common problems a person is exhibiting:

1. EMOTIONAL PROBLEMS

"When you follow the desires of your sinful nature, the results are very clear: sexual immorality, impurity, lustful pleasures, idolatry, sorcery, hostility, quarreling, **jealousy**, outbursts of **anger**, selfish ambition, dissension, division, **envy**, drunkenness, wild parties, and other sins like these. Let me tell you again, as I have before, that anyone living that sort of life will not inherit the Kingdom of God."
Galatians 5:19-21 NLT (emphasis added)

resentment	rejection	worry
hatred	self-pity	inferiority
anger	jealousy	insecurity
fear	depression	

Every negative emotion or attitude that we foster over a long period of time has the potential to open the way for a demon whose name corresponds with the same emotion. This demon can be called out directly as a spirit of [fill in the blank with any of the aforementioned emotions]. This is a truth for the remaining categories, as well.

2. MENTAL PROBLEMS

"A double minded man is unstable in all his ways."
James 1:8

| | | unbelief |
| | doubt | confusion |

forgetfulness	insanity	rationalization
indecision	mental	memory loss
compromise	torment	double-minded*
humanism	procrastination	

humanism: n. a variety of ethical theory and practice that emphasizes reason, scientific inquiry, and human fulfillment in the natural world and often rejects the importance of belief in God; a system of thought that rejects religious beliefs and centers on humans and our values, capacities, and worth

rationalize: vb. to ascribe one's acts, opinions, etc. to causes that superficially seem reasonable and valid but that actually are unrelated to the true (possibly unconscious and often less creditable or agreeable) causes

The mind is the battlefield of the human personality. It is one-third of what comprises the soul. Hence, to attack and attach to the mind is to breach the soul itself.

SPEECH PROBLEMS

"But the tongue can no man tame; it is an unruly evil, full of deadly poison."
James 3:8

lying	blasphemy	railing
cursing	criticism	gossip
	mockery	

rail(ing): vb. to utter bitter complaint or vehement denunciation

blasphemy: n. an absolute denouncing of God the

Father, Son and/or Holy Ghost (the latter of which is listed as the one unforgiveable sin in Matthew 12:32)

The third chapter of the book of James describes the tongue as a world of fire and iniquity (see verse 6). It goes on to describe its functionality as a state of double-mindedness for its propensity to bless God and curse man (made in the image and likeness of God) and likens it to a brook that produces both sweet and bitter water (how can this be?). Speech problems denote a heart problem as John 6:45 informs us that the mouth speaks out of the abundance of the heart. And since people of antiquity attributed the heart to be the same as the mind (not in a physical sense), how a man uses his mouth speaks to the state of his mind. As such, those that lack the ability to control their mouths prove themselves to be a lover of the fruit thereof which yields the power of death:

> "Death and life are in the power of the tongue: and they that love it shall eat the fruit thereof."
> **Proverbs 18:21**
>
> "There is that speaketh like the piercings of a sword: but the tongue of the wise is health."
> **Proverbs 12:18**
>
> "For by thy words thou shalt be justified, and by thy words thou shalt be condemned."
> **Matthew 12:37**

The reality is that we can open the door to demonic occupation by simply saying the wrong thing which can become a word curse. For example, compulsive (or habitual) liars are not aware of the lying demon they are entertaining and aligning within them. Not only can someone place you in bondage or judgment through words of condemnation, you can do the same to someone else! Once this alignment is fortified, a demon can either speak to a person's mind or through a person's tongue. But we have the power to cancel the wrong things out of the mouth by first repenting of what was said and then saying the right thing such as confessing the name and power of Jesus Christ – this is why nothing we say can move a demon to be cast out unless it's coupled with the mighty name of Jesus!

4. SEXUAL PROBLEMS

"For all that is in the world, the lust of the flesh, and the lust of the eyes, and the pride of life, is not of the Father, but is of the world." **I John 2:16**

sexual fantasy	lust	incest
pornography	homosexuality	provocativeness
masturbation	fornication	harlotry
	adultery	

As I John 2:16 states, these specific demons often enter through the eye gates to become the foundation for recurring unclean thoughts and actions. This is often the voluntary aspect of sexual problems when a person willfully chooses to expose themselves by stimulating their flesh for what may start off as entertainment purposes. However, there is a more insidious entry point for this type of predatory problem. If you haven't figured this out by now – the devil does not play fair. He is also very patient, it would seem. Sexual problems can have deep and involuntary origins – rooted in sexual abuse stemming from a person's childhood. Once the hooks are in (and there's no spiritual counsel/comfort offered to victims of sexual child abuse), the symptoms above manifest as a coping mechanism from a preexisting and unresolved condition which many people bury down deep inside (in darkness). From there, the enemy has fortified himself well and can be quite defensive. This is why confession (not of a crime but simply admitting the thoughts and/or actions) is often the biggest way to begin this particular deliverance process.

5. ADDICTION PROBLEMS

> "You say, 'I am allowed to do anything' – but not everything is good for you. And even though 'I am allowed to do anything,' I must not become a slave to anything." **I Corinthians 6:12 NLT**

nicotine	prescriptions	caffeine
cigarettes	coffee	white sugar
alcohol	drugs (opioids, cocaine, etc.)	food

Moderation is the key to consumption. Yet the spirits we're actively casting out of our bodies are ravenous! An appetite for destruction is more than just a song by Guns N' Roses! It's a lifestyle that directly contradicts the principle of self-control which, when correctly fostered, allows us to govern ourselves accordingly. We've even been given the fruit of temperance/self-control as a means to cultivate a life that bears much of this and other good fruit (see Galatians 5:22-23).

6. PHYSICAL INFIRMITIES

> "Surely he hath borne our griefs, and carried our sorrows: yet we did esteem him stricken, smitten of God, and afflicted. But he was wounded for our transgressions, he was bruised for our iniquities: the chastisement of our peace was upon him; and with his stripes we are healed." **Isaiah 53:4-5**

arthritis   diseases   deformities

sickness   infections
cancers   disorders   disabilities

infirmity: n. physical weakness; disease, frailty

There are plenty of examples in the Bible of people afflicted by unclean spirits that receive healing as a part of the package deal along with deliverance (see Luke 6:18, 13:11; Mark 9:17-29). However, I do want to note that not every physical disease is associated to demonic activity. There are external (environmental) factors that cause us to be sick but, at the same time, other sicknesses are induced by internal triggers from spiritual matters. Again, this is why the Holy Spirit's gift of discerning of spirits is so important.

7. RELIGIOUS ERROR

"Whosoever transgresseth, and abideth not in the doctrine of Christ, hath not God. He that abideth in the doctrine of Christ, he hath both the Father and the Son." **II John 1:9**

false religions   occultism   spiritism
false doctrines   (witchcraft)   Christian cults

spiritism: n. a belief that spirits of the dead communicate with the living usually through a medium

medium: n. a person through whom other persons try to communicate with the spirits of the dead (also known as a necromancer); possessor of a conjuring spirit with which the dead are conjured up for the purpose of inquiring about the future

conjure: vb. to summon by incantation

> **heresy** (from the Greek word *hairesis*): n. dissensions arising from diversity of opinions and aims
>
> **incantation**: n. a use of spells or verbal charms (spoken or sung) as a part of a ritual of magic
>
> **dissension**[2] (from the Greek word *stasis*) n. strife, disagreement

Simply stated, anything or person that teaches a way to commune with God the Father and Creator of all other than through Jesus Christ in such a way that it causes disunity and confusion in the Church body teaches religious error. Praying to dead saints is religious error. Invoking nature as an entity to be revered in and of itself is religious error. Denying the necessity of Christ's blood as atonement for sins is religious error. Following after another human being who claims to be the second coming of Jesus has proven to be religious error. Accessing the spiritual realm outside of the will of God as manifested in His Son Jesus and Holy Ghost is religious error (horoscopes, astrology, mediums, psychics, divination, astral projection and the like). A good example of such religious error can be referenced again by the girl who followed Paul around in Acts professing him to be a servant of God (see Acts 16:16-18).

> **divination**: n. the fortune telling practice of using the stars, tarot cards, tea leaves, crystal balls, horoscopes and palm reading to tell the future
>
> **astral projection**: n. the ability of a person to intentionally project their spirit to travel to distant places of their own will (outside of God's will)

"As I urged you when I went into Macedonia – remain in Ephesus that you may charge some that they teach no other doctrine, nor give heed to fables and endless genealogies, which cause disputes rather than godly edification which is in faith." **I Timothy 1:3-4 NKJV**

"But there were also false prophets among the people, even as there will be false teachers among you, who will secretly bring in destructive heresies, even denying the Lord who bought them, and bring on themselves swift destruction." **I Peter 2:1 NKJV**

It feels obvious to say this but accessing spiritual matters outside of God's will is a recipe for demonic activity in our lives.

REFERENCES TO AND EXAMPLES OF DELIVERANCE

Matthew 10:1
(amplification added)

"And when he had called unto him twelve disciples, he gave them power (authority) against unclean spirits, to cast them out, and to heal all manner of sickness and all manner of disease."

Mark 3:13-15
(amplification added)

"And he goeth up into as mountain, and calleth unto him whom he would: and they came unto him. And he ordained twelve, that they should be with him, and that he might send them forth to preach and to have power (authority) to heal sickness, and to cast out devils:"

Luke 9:1-2

"Then he called his twelve disciples together, and gave them power and authority over all devils, and to cure diseases. And he sent them to preach the kingdom of God, and to heal the sick."

Matthew 12:28-29

"But if I cast out devils by the Spirit of God, then the kingdom of God is come upon you. Or else how can one enter into a strong's mans house, and spoil his goods, except he first bind the strong man, and then he will spoil his house."

Luke 8:26-35
(other Gospel accounts of the demon-possessed man: Matthew 8:28-32, Mark 5:1-15)

"And they arrived at the country of the Gadarenes, which is over against Galilee. And when he went forth to land, there met him out of the city a certain man, which had devils long time, and ware no clothes, neither abode in any house, but in the tombs. When he saw Jesus, he cried out, and fell down before him, and with a loud voice said, What have I to do with thee, Jesus, thou Son of God most high? I beseech thee, torment me not. (For he had commanded the unclean spirit to come out of the man. For oftentimes it had caught him: and he was kept bound with chains and in fetters; and he brake the bands, and was driven of the devil into the wilderness.) And Jesus asked him, saying, What is thy name? And he said,

Legion: because many devils were entered into him. And they besought him that he would not command them to go out into the deep. And there was there an herd of many swine feeding on the mountain: and they besought him that he would suffer them to enter into them. And he suffered them. Then went the devils out of the man, and entered into the swine: and the herd ran violently down a steep place into the lake, and were choked. When they that fed them saw what was done, they fled, and went and told it in the city and in the country. Then they went out to see what was done; and came to Jesus, and found the man, out of whom the devils were departed, sitting at the feet of Jesus, clothed, and in his right mind: and they were afraid."

PREPARING FOR YOUR DELIVERANCE

As you renew your mind concerning your need for deliverance, please consider the following steps:

1. <u>Affirm Your Faith in Christ Personally</u>

"Wherefore, holy brethren, partakers of the heavenly calling, consider the Apostle and High Priest of our profession (confession even), Christ Jesus." **Hebrews 3:1 (amplification added)**

We must make our mouths agree with the Word of God. If we fail to confess our faith in this way, we give Jesus no basis on which to intervene for us.

> **confess**[1] (from the Greek word *homologeo;* a compound word formed from the words *homo* and *logos*): vb. to say the same words as

2. <u>Humble Yourself</u>

"Therefore humble yourselves under the mighty hand of God, that He may exalt you in due time,"
I Peter 5:6 NKJV

God never offers to make us humble; he places the responsibility on us. However, God can humiliate us sometimes when He must if we are not willing to make ourselves humble. (see Matthew 26:34, 69-75)

When seeking deliverance there may come a time when you will have to choose between dignity and deliverance. And, if dignity is more important than deliverance, then you've not repented of your pride (which naturally opposes humility).

3. <u>Confess Any Known Sin</u>

"If we confess our sins, he is faithful and just to forgive us our sins, and to cleanse us from all unrighteousness. If we say that we have not sinned, we make him a liar, and his word is not in us."
I John 1:9-10

> **confess**[2] (from the Greek word *homologeo*): vb. to admit or declare one's self guilty of what one is accused of

"He that covereth his sins shall not prosper: but whoso confesseth and forsaketh them shall have mercy." **Proverbs 28:13**

Repentance involves two things: accepting responsibility for what you did and then taking a stand against your sin. Don't minimize or excuse it –

hate it. Forsake it. It caused you to be separated from your Father and brought about the death of Jesus in your place (see Romans 6:23). Be honest when you confess it; don't call it something that it's not. Most sins are against someone else other than God. He knows your sins so you ought not seek Him out in your confession. He was there, after all! Seek out the person whom you sinned against or whom you least want to know about your transgression. That's true confession (see James 5:16). Allow the Holy Spirit to help bring things to your remembrance. Repent of all sins.

4. <u>Forgive People As You've Received Forgiveness</u>

"And when ye stand praying, forgive, if ye have ought against any: that your Father also which is in heaven may forgive you your trespasses. And when ye stand praying, forgive, if ye have ought against any: that your Father also which is in heaven may forgive you your trespasses." **Mark 11:25-26**

> **forgive** (from the Greek word *apheimi*): vb. to send; to send forth; to give up a debt; in various applications: - cry, forgive, forsake, lay aside, leave, omit, put (send) away, remit, suffer, yield up
>
> **SPECIAL NOTE**: Forgiveness of sin and cleansing from sin are two different things:
>
> 1. Forgiveness is to pardon; to cancel a debt
>
> 2. Cleansing is to free from dirt so as to become unsoiled, unstained; free from pollution; pure, unstained with the guilt of anything

So then, unforgiveness is everything forgiveness is

not. It is NOT sending away. NOT laying aside. NOT letting alone. NOT letting go. NOT giving up someone else's debt. Unforgiveness can come from being hurt, rejected, abandoned, disappointed, abused, raped, molested, lied on, taken advantage of, talked about, etc. As the list goes on and on, the stronghold builds higher and higher as the unclean spirits get stronger and stronger.

When you don't forgive, you retain the offender's sin(s) in your body and soul. An inability to forgive shows what's remained in your heart (resentment, bitterness indignation from been treated unfairly); often from the moment a person violates you – no matter how long ago it was. It's as the old adage goes: refusing to forgive is like drinking poison and expecting the other person to die. Only this poison can harm both the body and soul because an unforgiving heart not only robs you of your health; it also robs you of the blessings of the Lord and answered prayers.

There is perhaps no greater scripture in the gospels that attests to the connection between the need for deliverance and forgiveness than the parable of the unforgiving servant. While Matthew 18:23-35 is familiar to most, there is a subtle reference to deliverance that is often overlooked in verses 34-35:

> "And his lord was wroth, and delivered him to the tormentors, till he should pay all that was due unto him. So likewise shall my heavenly Father do also unto you, if ye from your hearts forgive not every one his brother their trespasses."

You see, after the lord of the story hears how the servant whose substantial debt he had forgiven was unwilling to forgive the trivial debt of another servant, the lord turned him over to tormentors. Unforgiveness is the legality that demons use to gain access to you. Any unforgiveness that you have towards someone else pales in comparison to the sin debt Jesus bought and forgave of you; so, to withhold forgiveness from someone else (a fellowservant) in light of what you've been forgiven leaves you vulnerable to spiritual oppression. The demons know how to maneuver within this principle… it's high time we learned how to maneuver around it. Forgive.

> "Whose soever sins ye remit, they are remitted unto them; and whose soever sins ye retain, they are retained." **John 20:23**

5. <u>Break with the Occult and All False Religion</u>

"And he caused his children to pass through the fire in the valley of the son of Hinnom: also he observed times, and used enchantments, and used witchcraft, and dealt with a familiar spirit, and with wizards: he wrought much evil in the sight of the LORD, to provoke him to anger." **II Chronicles 33:6**

Eastern philosophies (though highly spiritual) are highly false. Approaches such as psychics, wicca, voodoo and freemasonry provide illegal access (circumventing Christ the Lord and God the Father) to heavenly matters. Lurking somewhere in the background of all this is the archenemy of God. If you want to draw closer to God, you must sever all contact with the devil.

6. <u>Prepare to Be Released from Every Curse Over Your Life</u>

"Thou shalt not bow down thyself to them, nor serve them: for I the LORD thy God am a jealous God, visiting the iniquity of the fathers upon the children unto the third and fourth generation of them that hate me;" **Exodus 20:5**

"Thou shalt not bow down thyself unto them, nor serve them: for I the LORD thy God am a jealous God, visiting the iniquity of the fathers upon the children unto the third and fourth generation of them that hate me, And shewing mercy unto thousands of them that love me and keep my commandments." **Deuteronomy 5:9-10**

You know it's serious when God all but restates Himself verbatim more than once! What's playing out in the previous scriptures are generational curses. Actions of our blood relatives have often given the enemy legal grounds on which to attack. Be prepared to forgive and intercede on behalf of your forefathers for the curses they exposed you to as Nehemiah did (see Nehemiah 9:2). Be prepared to renounce and denounce the things you've been positioned to come into alignment with – both known and unknown. The Holy Spirit can discern this for you. I often speak Daniel 9:4-19 to renounce a curse once it's been uncovered.

Here are signs of possible curses operating in your family lineage:

- Mental or Emotional Breakdowns
- Chronic Sickness
- Barrenness
- Dysfunctional Family
- Financial Instability/Lack
- Suicides
- Unnatural or Untimely Death

    denounce: vb. to announce or proclaim something evil or calamitous

>   **renounce**: vb. to give up or put aside voluntarily; to disown

7. <u>Take Your Stand with God</u>

"Put on the whole armour of God, that ye may be able to stand against the wiles of the devil."
Ephesians 6:11

When you take your stand with God, He will take His stand with you. Taking a stand is not a passive thing. It is not standing still. It is actively working against the powers of evil; pushing it back so that the gates of hell do not prevail as we actively advance God's Kingdom using the resources He's made available to us. Deliverance, like ALL Kingdom work on earth, is a partnership between us and God. As we do the work (making full proof of our ministry), He will *continue* to do a work in us!

HOW TO MAINTAIN YOUR DELIVERANCE

Maintenance has to do with upkeeping the existing state of a thing. It can also mean to continue in or preserve from failure/decline. Maintaining stresses firmness of conviction as something has been set in a new direction. Deliverance sets the believer in a new direction concerning a particular area in your life. Specifically, an area that was once maligned with darkness.

Recalling that an unclean spirit will attempt to return to the person it was cast out from, it's important to remember that such spirits gain entry through gates where sin is active in our lives. This is much of the demonic activity on our planet: demons roaming around looking for a way to get back into our lives.

Be Aware of Your Surroundings

"And the Lord said unto Satan, whence comest thou? Then Satan answered the Lord and said, From going to and fro in the earth, and from walking up and down in it." **Job 1:7**

"When the unclean spirit is gone out of a man, he walketh through dry places, seeking rest, and findeth none. Then he saith, I will return into my house from whence I came out; and when he is come, he findeth it empty, swept, and garnished. Then goeth he, and taketh with himself seven other spirits more wicked than himself, and they enter in and dwell there: and the last state of that man is worse than the first. Even so shall it be also unto this wicked generation."
Matthew 12:43-45

"When the unclean spirit is gone out of a man, he walketh through dry places, seeking rest; and finding none, he saith, I will return unto my house whence I came out. And when he cometh, he findeth it swept and garnished. Then goeth he, and taketh to him seven other spirits more wicked than himself; and they enter in, and dwell there: and the last state of that man is worse than the first." **Luke 11:24-26**

"Be sober, be vigilant; because your adversary the devil, as a roaring lion, walketh about, seeking whom he may devour: whom resist steadfast in the faith, knowing that the same afflictions are accomplished in your brethren that are in the world." **I Peter 5:8-9**

sober: adj. calm and collected in spirit; temperate (marked by moderation); dispassionate (not influenced by strong feeling, not affected by personal or emotional involvement); circumspect (careful to consider all circumstances and possible consequences)

vigilant: adj. watchful; given to strict attention; cautious, active; heedful lest some destructive calamity suddenly overtake a person

"…behold, Satan hath desired to have you that he may sift you as wheat:" **Luke 22:31b**

Fortify Your Soul:
Repair the Breach, Rebuild the Walls

"Let us not sleep, as do others; but let us watch and be sober." **I Thessalonians 5:6**

"He that hath no rule over his own spirit is like a city that is broken down, and without walls." **Proverbs 25:28**

"Let the priests take it to them, every man of his acquaintance: and let them repair the breaches of the house, wheresoever any breach shall be found." **II Kings 12:5**

"A wholesome tongue is a tree of life: but perverseness therein is a breach in the spirit." **Proverbs 15:4**

"Therefore this iniquity shall be to you as a breach ready to fall, swelling out in a high wall, whose breaking cometh suddenly at an instant." **Isaiah 30:13**

"And they that shall be of thee shall build the old waste places: thou shalt raise up the foundations of many generations; and thou shalt be called, The repairer of the breach, The restorer of paths to dwell in."
Isaiah 58:12

Sin No More

"Afterward Jesus findeth him in the temple, and said unto him, Behold, thou art made whole: sin no more, lest a worse thing come unto thee." **John 5:14**

"Afterward Jesus findeth him in the temple, and said unto him, Behold, thou art made whole: sin no more, lest a worse thing come unto thee. She said, No man, Lord. And Jesus said unto her, Neither do I condemn thee: go, and sin no more." **John 8:10-11**

"For if after they have escaped the pollutions of the world through the knowledge of the Lord and Saviour Jesus Christ, they are again entangled therein, and overcome, the latter end is worse with them than the beginning." **II Peter 2:20**

"When you follow the desires of your sinful nature, the results are very clear: sexual immorality, impurity, lustful pleasures, idolatry, sorcery, hostility, quarreling, jealousy, outbursts of anger, selfish ambition, dissension, division, envy, drunkenness, wild parties, and other sins like these. Let me tell you again, as I have before, that anyone living that sort of life will not inherit the Kingdom of God." **Galatians 5:19-21 NLT**

> **dissension**[1] (from the Greek word *dichostasia*): n. division

sorcery (from the Greek word *pharmakeia* which is where the word pharmacy is derived from): n. magical arts induced through drugs, alcohol, suggestive dancing, charms or wearing ancestral/ancient makeup

"Temptation comes from our own desires, which entice us and drag us away. These desires give birth to sinful actions. And when sin is allowed to grow, it gives birth to death." **James 1:14-15**

Fill Your House

1. Live by the Word of God

Everything you think, say, and do should reflect you living no other way than by the word of God. Give it unchallenged preeminence in every area of your life. Though other things will compete for control (emotions, opinions, accepted traditions, culture, etc.), prioritize the Word of God above all else. Think the Word. Speak the Word. Act out the Word.

> "But he answered and said, It is written, Man shall not live by bread alone, but by every word that proceedeth out of the mouth of God."
> **Matthew 4:4**
> (also see Luke 4:4 and Deuteronomy 8:3)

> "This book of the law shall not depart out of thy mouth; but thou shalt meditate therein day and night, that thou mayest observe to do according to all that is written therein: for then thou shalt make thy way prosperous, and then thou shalt have good success." **Joshua 1:8**

2. Put on the Garment of Praise

When you begin to enter into praise (honoring God for what He's done in your life) and worship (honoring God for Who He is), you trouble the devil more than he could ever trouble you.

> "To appoint unto them that mourn in Zion to give them beauty for ashes, the oil of joy for mourning, the garment of praise for the spirit of heaviness..."
> **Isaiah 61:3a-d**

> "But thou art holy, O thou that inhabitest the praises of Israel. Our fathers trusted in thee: they trusted, and thou didst deliver them."
> **Psalm 22:3-4**

3. <u>Come Under Discipline</u>

Learn to discipline yourself. Bring your emotions, desires and appetites under control. God requires us to cultivate submissiveness in all areas of our lives and affords us the means to do so with the fruit of the Spirit of self-control/temperance. Though it may sound contradictory, we actually become free when we bring every area of our lives under the discipline of God. Refusing to completely submit to such discipline is an act of defiance and rebellion.

Rebellion against God is as the sin of witchcraft because it exposed our entire race to the deceptive and destructive power of Satan (see I Samuel 15:23). We come under God's protection as we place ourselves under His discipline. Consequently, an undisciplined life is a life that is vulnerable to demonic attack.

> **cultivate**: n. to foster the growth of; to loosen or break up the soil about (growing plants i.e. fruit)

discipline: n. training to act in accordance with rules

disciple: n. one who is under discipline; a pupil, learner

"He openeth also their ear to discipline, and commandeth that they return from iniquity." **Job 36:10**

"Go therefore and make disciples of all the nations, baptizing them in the name of the Father and of the Son and of the Holy Spirit, teaching them to observe all things that I have commanded you; and lo, I am with you always, even to the end of the age." Amen." **Matthew 28:19-20 NKJV**

"for God did not give us a spirit of timidity but a spirit of power and love and self-control." **II Timothy 1:7 RSV**

"For God has not given us a spirit of fear and timidity, but of power, love, and self-discipline." **II Timothy 1:7 NLT**

4. Fellowship: Cultivate the Right Relationships

Recognize the most powerful influences in our lives are the people we associate with. We must choose the kinds of people we spend time with.
    fellowship: (from the Greek word *koinonia*) n. association, community, communion, joint participation

"Behold, how good and how pleasant it is for brethren to dwell together in unity!" **Psalm 133:1**

"Be not deceived: evil communications corrupt good manners." **I Corinthians 15:33**

"But if we walk in the light, as he is in the light, we have fellowship one with another, and the blood of Jesus Christ his Son cleanseth us from all sin." **I John 1:7**

"...and let us consider how to stir up one another to love and good works, not neglecting to meet together, as is the habit of some, but encouraging one another, and all the more as you see the Day drawing near." **Hebrew 10:24-25 RSV**

5. <u>Be Filled with the Holy Spirit</u>

Being filled with the Holy Spirit is an essential part of living victoriously. As such, it would do us well to define the Holy Spirit which is what this book dives into in the next chapter.

CHAPTER 5:
THE HOLY SPIRIT

WHO Is The Holy Spirit?

As a spiritual being of the Godkind, The Holy Spirit is a member of The Godhead (or what others refer to as the Trinity):

- God the Father
- God the Son
- God the Holy Spirit

He is also referred to as The "Comforter" and "Spirit of Truth" sent in addition to another (Jesus) Who had already been sent:

> "And I will pray the Father, and he shall give you another Comforter, that he may abide with you forever; Even the Spirit of truth; whom the world cannot receive, because it seeth him not, neither knoweth him: but ye know him; for he dwelleth with you, and shall be in you."
> **John 14:16,17, 26**

As Comforter, the Holy Ghost soothes in time of affliction, distress, grief and fear. He relieves us physically as well as spiritually. He is our helper and our strength. He provides us power to resist spiritual attack. He gives us the ability to maintain a moral and intellectual position. He is a supportive and protective power.

"God is a Spirit: and they that worship him must worship him in spirit and in truth." **John 4:24**

"Now the Lord is that Spirit: and where the Spirit of the Lord is, there is liberty." **II Corinthians 3:17**

"Howbeit when he, the Spirit of truth, is come, he will guide you into all truth: for he shall not speak of himself; but whatsoever he shall hear, that shall he speak: and he will shew you things to come." **John 16:13**

WHAT Is The Holy Spirit?

The Holy Spirit is God's power living in and among those that believe. The title "Holy Spirit" (or "Holy Ghost") is taken from the Greek phrase *hagios pneuma* where:

- *hagios* means "holy" or "sacred"

- *pneuma* means "breath," "breathe," "life" or "spirit"

Though these words are in the New Testament, "breathe" recalls to mind God's action in the Old Testament which made man a living soul:

> "And the LORD God formed man of the dust of the ground, and **breathed** into his nostrils the breath of life; and man became a **living soul**." **Genesis 2:7 (emphasis added)**

"And when he had said this, he breathed on them, and saith unto them, Receive ye the Holy Ghost:" **John 20:22**

What Does the Holy Spirit Do?

The Holy Spirit does much for us and through us! He soothes in times of affliction and distress. He relieves us physically. He helps us by comforting us in times of grief and fear. He is also our strength. He provides us power to resist spiritual attack. He gives us the ability to maintain a moral and intellectual position. He is a supportive and protective power.

I once heard that Jesus came to earth to bring God to us while the Holy Ghost came to earth to bring God *through* us! Here are some ways in which the Holy Spirit acts this out:

He Will Be with Us Forever	John 14:16
The World Cannot Accept Him	John 14:17
He Teaches Us	John 14:26
He Lives with and In Us	Luke 17:21
He Reminds Us of Jesus' Words	John 15:26
He Convicts of Sin	John 16:8
He Guides Us into Truth	John 16:13
He Brings Glory to Christ	John 16:14

The Holy Spirit Transforms Us from Within

The Holy Spirit is the very presence of God and His Kingdom dwelling within us; helping us to live as God wants as we build up the Church on earth. Christ prayed that we would receive the Holy Spirit as another Comforter and that He would abide and dwell with us forever (see John 14:16-17). This indwelling is not as much a bodily sense as it is a principle of being in union with us within a covenant of agreement we have in Christ Jesus.

> **abide**: vb. to stay in a given place, state, relation, to remain in a place

> **indwelling**: n. the permanent presence of God or a spiritual force in the heart or soul; an existence as an animating or divine inner spirit, force, or principle

> **animate**: vb. to give or fill with life; to impart interest or zest to; to enliven or make lively; to give the quality or condition of being alive, active or vigorous; to fill with spirit, courage or resolution; to inspire to action; to impart motion or activity to; to cause to possess life

Though we don't begin to hear about God's Holy Spirit dwelling within us until Jesus sends Him, there is a precedent for this as part of God's will that can be found in the Old Testament, as well... apparently, Ezekiel was on to something!:

> "And the spirit entered into me when he spake unto me, and set me upon my feet, that I heard him that spake unto me." **Ezekiel 2:2**

> "Then the spirit entered into me, and set me upon my feet, and spake with me, and said unto me, Go, shut thyself within thine house." **Ezekiel 3:24**

> "A new heart also will I give you, and a new spirit will I put within you: and I will take away the stony heart out of your flesh, and I will give you an heart of flesh. And I will put my spirit within you, and cause you to walk in my statutes, and ye shall keep my judgments, and do them." **Ezekiel 36:26-27**

> **statute**: n. an established law or regulation: an authoritative order or proclamation issued by an authority and having the force of law

> **judgment**: n. an ability to make decisions or evaluations that are wise, reasonable and valid; a verdict pronounced judicially, especially a sentence or formal decree

<u>New Testament Examples of Dwelling in Union:</u>

God in Christ	II Corinthians 5:19
Christ in God	John 14:20
Christ in Man	Colossians 1:27
God and Christ in Each Other	John 14:10-11
Man and Christ in Each Other	John 14:20
Man and Spirit in Each Other	Romans 8:9-10
Man in the Father and Son	I John 2:24
Man in Christ	II Corinthians 5:17

>**in union (with)**: adv. consecrated to the same end; one in mind, purpose and life; joined as in the covenant of marriage

"But he that is joined unto the Lord is one spirit." **I Corinthians 6:17**

"That they all may be one; as thou, Father, art in me, and I in thee, that they also may be one in us: that the world may believe that thou hast sent me. And the glory which thou gavest me I have given them; that they may be one, even as we are one: I in them, and thou in me, that they may be made perfect in one; and that the world may know that thou hast sent me, and hast loved them, as thou hast loved me." **John 17:21-23**

The Holy Spirit Empowers Believers

The Holy Spirit enables or empowers us with a supernatural ability; He increases us in mental and physical strength for special tasks. The task at hand as it relates to this book is deliverance!

>**power** (from the Greek word *dynamis*): n. strength power, ability, power residing within a thing by

virtue of its nature or which a person or thing exerts and puts forth; power whether by virtue of one's own ability and resources, or of state of mind, or through favorable circumstances, or by permission of law or custom; miraculous power: ability, might; (worker of) power, strength, mighty works; the word "dynamite" stems from this word

empower(ment): n. a temporary and spontaneous increase of physical and spiritual or mental strength

"And, behold, I send the promise of my Father upon you: but tarry ye in the city of Jerusalem, until ye be endued with power from on high." **Luke 24:49**

"But ye shall receive power, after that the Holy Ghost is come upon you: and ye shall be witnesses unto me both in Jerusalem, and in all Judaea, and in Samaria, and unto the uttermost part of the earth." **Acts 1:8**

"Great is our Lord, and of great power: his understanding is infinite." **Psalm 147:5**

"The LORD is slow to anger, and great in power," **Nahum 1:3a**

"But truly I am full of power by the spirit of the LORD, and of judgment, and of might, to declare unto Jacob his transgression, and to Israel his sin." **Micah 3:8**

"Behold, I give unto you power(authority) to tread on serpents and scorpions, and over all the power of the enemy: and nothing shall by any means hurt you." **Luke 10:19**

"Verily, verily, I say unto you, He that believeth on me, the works that I do shall he do also; and greater works than these shall he do; because I go unto my Father." **John 14:12**

The Power Christ Possesses

So, if the Holy Spirit enables or empowers us with supernatural ability... what should we do with it? I'll answer a question with a question: Why did Jesus need the Holy Spirit to perform works as the Son of God? Let's not forget that He was known as the Son of Man, as well. The signs, wonders, miracles and healings that Christ performed were all strengths He received once the Holy Spirit enabled Him!:

> "And Jesus, when he was baptized, went up straightway out of the water: and, lo, the heavens were opened unto him, and he saw the Spirit of God descending like a dove, and lighting upon him:" **Matthew 3:16**

> "And straightway coming up out of the water, he saw the heavens opened, and the Spirit like a dove descending upon him:" **Mark 1:10**

> "And John bare record, saying, I saw the Spirit descending from heaven like a dove, and it abode upon him. And I knew him not: but he that sent me to baptize with water, the same said unto me, Upon whom thou shalt see the Spirit descending, and remaining on him, the same is he which baptizeth with the Holy Ghost." **John 1:32-33**

It's not a coincidence that Jesus launched into His ministry full of power and might shortly after this account. Wo/Man of God, your ministry must launch forward with power after receiving the Holy Spirit, as well!

After all, the fruit and gifts in Galatians 5 and I Corinthians 12 aren't the fruit and gifts of Jesus, but the Fruit and Gifts of the... say it with me... HOLY GHOST! The same Spirit that abided with Jesus dwells within us which is why He says (with confidence) in John 14:12 that we are meant to do greater works than He!

"Then Peter said unto them, Repent, and be baptized every one of you in the name of Jesus Christ for the remission of sins, and ye shall receive the gift of the Holy Ghost." **Act 2:38**

"But the manifestation of the Spirit is given to every man to profit withal." **1 Corinthians 12:7**

"The Holy Spirit displays God's power through each of us as a means of helping the entire church."
1 Corinthians 12:7 TLB

CHAPTER 6:
RESTORATION OF THE FRAGMENTED SOUL

"And the Lord God formed man of the dust of the ground, and breathed into his nostrils the breath of life; and man became a living soul." **Genesis 2:7**

"The spirit of God hath made me, and the breath of the Almighty hath given me life." **Job 33:4**

"The first man Adam was made a living soul; the last Adam was made a life-giving spirit."
I Corinthians 15:45

We've spoken of the soul throughout this book thus far but it deserves more direct attention. When we speak about deliverance, we're talking about the state of our souls. Remembering that the spirit of the believer who has confessed "Jesus is Lord" is perfected and seated in Christ in heavenly places, what remains here in our earthly bodies is the soul (see Ephesians 2:5-6). Even Hebrews 4:12 separates the soul and spirit – distinguishable by none other than the Word of God (otherwise known as Jesus)!:

> "For the word of God is quick, and powerful, and sharper than any twoedged sword, **piercing even to the dividing asunder of soul and spirit**, and of the joints and marrow, and is a discerner of the thoughts and intents of the heart."
> **(emphasis added)**

Further still, I Thessalonians 5:23 brings an important characteristic into play as it relates to the spirit versus the soul:

> "And the very God of peace sanctify you wholly; and I pray God your whole spirit and soul and body be preserved blameless unto the coming of our Lord Jesus Christ."

> **wholly** (from the Greek word *holoteles*): adj. complete to the end, that is, absolutely perfect

Do you see that?!! God is complete. We (our souls) are not. God is absolutely perfect. There is neither nothing missing nor nothing broken in God; partly because His Word cannot return to Him void (see Isaiah 55:11). We, on the other hand?!! Does it take much effort to remember the last time you said you would do something but didn't follow your words up with the appropriate action to complete it? If you're like me, that's happened more times than you'd care to admit! Something as simple as not keeping your word fragments who you are here on earth which can impact your integrity or *wholeness*.

> **fragment**: n. a part broken away from a whole; broken pieces; a detached, isolated or incomplete part; disconnected

> **integrity**: n. the quality or state of being complete; the condition of being free from damage or defect

Granted, this is just one example to illustrate the simple fact that the soul is fragmented: a part broken away from the whole (spirit). In truth, the soul has many angles to approach its fragmentation as it consists of three components: the mind, the will and the emotions:

> **mind** (from the Greek word *nous*): n. the seat of reflective consciousness, comprising the facilities of perception and understanding and those of feeling, judging, determining; the intellective faculty; reason

>> "I will praise thee; for I am fearfully and wonderfully made; marvelous are thy works;

and that my soul knoweth right well."
Psalm 139:14

"Also, that the soul be without knowledge, it is not good;" **Proverbs 19:2a-b**

will (from the Greek word *thelema*): n. what one wishes or has determined to be done; choice, inclination, desire, pleasure

"And I will say to my soul, Soul, thou hast much goods laid up for many years; take thine ease, eat, drink, and be merry."
Luke 12:19

"In whom also we have obtained an inheritance, being predestinated according to the purpose of him who worketh all things after the counsel of his own will:"
Ephesians 1:11

"Then thou scarest me with dreams, and terrifiest me through visions: So that my soul chooseth strangling, and death rather than my life." **Job 7:14-15**

emotion(s): n. a conscious mental reaction (as anger or fear) individually experienced as strong feeling usually directed toward a specific object or person and typically accompanied by physical and behavioral changes in the body

"But if ye will not hear it, my soul shall weep in secret places for your pride; and mine eye shall weep sore, and run down with tears, because the LORD'S flock is carried away captive." **Jeremiah 13:17**

> "And my soul shall be joyful in the LORD: it shall rejoice in his salvation." **Psalm 35:9**

> "Tell me, O thou whom my soul loveth," **Song of Solomon 1:7a**

When part of the soul has been broken or isolated from the whole, a person's capacity to love and magnify the Lord becomes less stable. Unstable souls aren't grounded in the word and are capable of being beguiled.

> **beguile**: vb. to seduce, trick, dupe (see the SEDUCERS Section in CHAPTER 2)

When part of the soul is broken, a person's ability to love others is reduced. Not only that, but the ability to love and magnify the Lord is reduced as well which means the Creator is robbed of His just due. How so? I'm glad you asked! If a person lost just one-third of his/her soul, that person is only capable of loving the Lord at two-thirds of his/her full capacity. How much of ourselves are we supposed to love God with – what does Jesus tell us in Matthew 22:37-39 (which is a reference to the Old Testament)?:

> "Jesus said unto him, Thou shalt love the Lord thy God with all thy heart, and with all thy soul, and with all thy mind. This is the first and great commandment. And the second is like unto it, Thou shalt love thy neighbour as thyself."

> "And now Israel, what doth the Lord thy God require of thee, but to fear the Lord thy God, to walk in all his ways, and to love him, and to serve the Lord thy God will all they heart and with all thy soul," **Deuteronomy 10:12**

Since the soul is not as secured in Christ Jesus as the spirit is (see John 10:28-30), our vulnerability to demonic attack increases. Once the soul has been compromised, an unclean spirit's sole objective is to destroy it. Why? They honestly have no just cause besides the fact that misery loves company. And since demons know their time on earth is 1) limited and 2) set to end in fiery destruction, they want to take out whomever takes after (looks like) the Source of their destruction; especially those made in His image and likeness.

> "For without cause have they hid for me their net in a pit, which without cause they have digged for my soul." **Psalm 35:7**

> "For mine enemies speak against me; and they that lay wait for my soul take counsel together, Saying, God hath forsaken him: persecute and take him; for there is none to deliver him. O God, be not far from me: O my God, make haste for my help. Let them be confounded and consumed that are adversaries to my soul; let them be covered with reproach and dishonour that seek my hurt." **Psalm 71:10-13**

> "They gather themselves together, they hide themselves, they mark my steps, when they wait for my soul." **Psalm 56:6**

> "For, lo, they lie in wait for my soul: the mighty are gathered against me; not for my transgression, nor for my sin, O LORD." **Psalm 59:3**

> "Let them be ashamed and confounded together that seek after my soul to destroy it; let them be driven backward and put to shame that wish me evil." **Psalm 40:14**

> "But those that seek my soul, to destroy it, shall go into the lower parts of the earth." **Psalm 63:9**

> "And of thy mercy cut off mine enemies, and destroy all them that afflict my soul: for I am thy servant." **Psalm 143:12**

Don't miss the language of the Bible! You should take it literally when at all possible. The last two scriptures from Psalms state that the soul can be destroyed. When a soul has been brought to ruin or corrupted, that is a form of destruction. Check out what Acts 15:24 says:

> "Forasmuch as we have heard, that certain which went out from us have trouble you with words, subverting your souls," **Acts 15:24a-b**

>> **subvert**: vb. to dismantle, overthrow, ravage or ravish (to seize and carry off by force) something already established; to overcome with emotions

According to this last scripture, the soul can be subverted by words: what you read, watch, hear and speak. Once such breaches occur, the soul becomes compromised and fragmented.

Though the soul of man is in control of his body; it is ordinarily dominated and controlled by Satan and his demonic forces until a person is reborn. However, even after salvation, the soul is in need of restoration and regeneration which is why God has given us His word, the Blood of Christ and the Holy Ghost to help do this.

Subverting or dismantling our souls causes us to revert back to the mindset we were in before we were saved. Simply put, subversion's purpose is to bring us back into bondage.

> "Bring my soul out of prison, that I may praise thy

name: the righteous shall compass me about; for thou shalt deal bountifully with me." **Psalm 142:7**

Even though this scripture promises us that we will be dealt with bountifully by our Father, He can only do so with the parts of our soul which we freely relinquish to Him. Until this happens fully, our souls are fragmented – partly released, partly bound.

The Fragmented Soul

Enemy strongholds of the mind, will and emotions which we do not surrender to God are what fragment our souls. As such, many of the strongholds briefly touched on in previous chapters of this book will reappear here with more scriptural evidence to prove their impact (in no specific order):

Sexual Sin, Soul Ties and Immorality

soul tie: n. unholy connections resulting from every unsanctioned sexual partner a person has had outside of marriage (whereas, within marriage, this type of connection is sanctioned and holy)

> **SPECIAL NOTE:** A soul tie can also be formed by joining forces or uniting for a common end which does not involve sexual intercourse. I Samuel 18:1 says that Jonathan was knit with the soul of David, and Jonathan loved him as his own soul.

immorality: n. not confirmed with accepted principles of right and wrong behavior (morals)

> "But whoso committeth adultery with a woman lacketh understanding: he that doeth it destroyeth his own soul." **Proverbs 6:32**

"What? know ye not that he which is joined to an harlot is one body? for two, saith he, shall be one flesh." **I Corinthians 6:16**

"And when Shechem the son of Hamor the Hivite, prince of the country, saw her, he took her, and lay with her, and defiled her. And his soul clave unto Dinah the daughter of Jacob, and he loved the damsel," **Genesis 34:2-3a-b**

"For even their women did change the natural use into that which is against nature: And likewise also the men, leaving the natural use of the woman, burned in their lust one toward another; men with men working that which is unseemly," **Romans 1:26b-27a-b**

Drugs and Alcohol

"Let us walk honestly, as in the day; not in rioting and drunkenness, not in chambering and wantonness, not in strife and envying." **Romans 13:13**

"Therefore let us not sleep, as do others; but let us watch and be sober." **I Thessalonians 5:6**

"Therefore, with minds that are alert and fully sober, set your hope on the grace to be brought to you when Jesus Christ is revealed at his coming." **I Peter 1:13 NIV**

"Be sober, be vigilant; because your adversary the devil, as a roaring lion, walketh about, seeking whom he may devour:" **I Peter 5:8**

Idolatry, Witchcraft (known or done by you or even unknown through your family)

> "Regard not them that have familiar spirits, neither seek after wizards, to be defiled by them: I am the LORD your God." **Leviticus 19:31**
>
> "And the soul that turneth after such as have familiar spirits, and after wizards, to go a whoring after them, I will even set my face against that soul, and will cut him off from among his people." **Leviticus 20:6**
>
> "Who changed the truth of God into a lie, and worshipped and served the creature more than the Creator, who is blessed for ever. Amen. For this cause God gave them up unto vile affections:" **Romans 1:25-26a**
>
> "There shall not be found among you any one that maketh his son or his daughter to pass through the fire, or that useth divination, or an observer of times, or an enchanter, or a witch, Or a charmer, or a consulter with familiar spirits, or a wizard, or a necromancer. For all that do these things are an abomination unto the LORD: and because of these abominations the LORD thy God doth drive them out from before thee." **Deuteronomy 18:10-12**

Religious Error (see the DISCERNING THE NEED FOR DELIVERANCE section in CHAPTER 4)

> "Wherefore the Lord said, Forasmuch as this people draw near me with their mouth, and with their lips do honour me, but have removed their heart far from me, and their fear toward me is

taught by the precept of men:" **Isaiah 29:13**

>**precept** (from the Hebrew word *mitzvah*): n. commandment

"This people draweth nigh unto me with their mouth, and honoureth me with their lips; but their heart is far from me. But in vain they do worship me, teaching for doctrines the commandments of men." **Matthew 15:8-9**

"For there are many unruly and vain talkers and deceivers, specially they of the circumcision: Whose mouths must be stopped, who subvert whole houses, teaching things which they ought not, for filthy lucre's sake." **Titus 1:10-11**

"Woe unto you, scribes and Pharisees, hypocrites! for ye devour widows' houses, and for a pretence make long prayer: therefore ye shall receive the greater damnation." **Matthew 23:14**

>**pretence** (or pretense): n. a claim made or implied especially: one not supported by fact

<u>Curses, Vows and Oaths</u> (spiritual vows and oaths made to anyone else other than God outside of marriage or made but not honored with God)

>"If a man vow a vow unto the LORD, or swear an oath to bind his soul with a bond; he shall not break his word, he shall do according to all that proceedeth out of his mouth." **Numbers 30:2**

>>**vow** (from the Hebrew word *nadar*): n. a promise

> **bond** (from the Hebrew word *ecar*): n. (legally) binding obligation

"When you make a vow to the Lord your God, you shall not be slack in paying it, for the Lord your God will surely require it of you, and slackness would be sin in you." **Deuteronomy 23:21-22 AMP**

> **Example**: Jephthah and his daughter (see Judges 11:29-39)

"And when it was day, certain of the Jews banded together, and bound themselves under a curse, saying that they would neither eat nor drink till they had killed Paul." **Acts 23:12**

"Be not rash with thy mouth, and let not thine heart be hasty to utter anything before God: for God is in heaven, and thou upon earth: therefore let thy words be few." **Ecclesiastes 5:2**

"When thou vowest a vow unto God, defer not to pay it; for he hath no pleasure in fools: pay that which thou hast vowed. Better is it that thou shouldest not vow, than that thou shouldest vow and not pay. Suffer not thy mouth to cause thy flesh to sin; neither say thou before the angel, that it was an error:" **Ecclesiastes 5:4-6a-b**

Offense and Unforgiveness

offence or offense (from the Greek word *skandalon*): n. a stumbling block, something against which causes a person to fall; a trap or snare causing one to fall or sin

As offense has not been directly addressed up to this point in the book, I'd like to take some time to unpack it here. Ultimately, offense is just another form of bait the devil uses to bring us into and keep us in captivity.

Often, those who are offended don't realize it because they are focused on the wrong that was done to them.

> **offended**: adj. outraged or insulted; suggests a deliberate cause of humiliation, hurt pride, pain or shame

Typically, offended people see themselves as victims; blaming the offender who hurt them for their current condition. In doing so, offended people justify and produce damaged fruit such as hurt, anger, jealousy, resentment, strife, bitterness, hatred and envy. One way the enemy keeps such a person (we've all been there) in an offended state is to keep the wound of the offense open with unforgiveness and nestled under pride. Such pride produces a shell to protect us from being hurt again; but one wo/man's shell is another spirit's stronghold.

> "Let all bitterness, and wrath, and anger, and clamour, and evil speaking, be put away from you, with all malice: And be ye kind one to another, tenderhearted, forgiving one another, even as God for Christ's sake hath forgiven you."
> **Ephesians 4:31-32**

> "Then said he unto the disciples, It is impossible but that offences will come: but woe unto him, through whom they come! It were better for him that a millstone were hanged about his neck, and he cast into the sea, than that he should offend one of these little ones. Take heed to yourselves: If thy brother trespass against thee, rebuke him; and if he repent, forgive him. And if he trespass

against thee seven times in a day, and seven times in a day turn again to thee, saying, I repent; thou shalt forgive him." **Luke 17:1-4**

A person's refusal to repent from our offense and forgive can make said person hostile and loveless. Once settled in, any attempts to rescue someone from such a place is often met with extreme defense mechanisms such as insults, all-out attacks (verbal and/or physical), wounding and even backsliding when confronted with a word of truth from the Bible. The final stage of offense often finds people in division (internal), separation (external), broken relationships and betrayal.

Divided and Conquered

Deliverance is the restoration of the soul. Yet and still, though we are desperate for it – it is not something that can happen all at once, lest it destroy us. Some spirits are so intricately bound to us, that to remove them all at once would leave us without a personality. This is why deliverance is actually a lifelong process that we all must submit to over time. It's not a one-and-done type of deal. There is a precedent for this in Deuteronomy 7:22-23 where God instructs the children of Israel not to dispossess everything from the Promised Land as they inhabit it or else they would risk straining the land:

> "And the LORD thy God will put out those nations before thee by little and little: thou mayest not consume them at once, lest the beasts of the field increase upon thee. But the LORD thy God shall deliver them unto thee, and shall destroy them with a mighty destruction, until they be destroyed."

He means to destroy every unclean spirit that has ever dared to ensnare us but the restoration is one that must be done over time as the land (our bodies) is given time to rest and recover.

> "Arise, O LORD, disappoint him, cast him down: deliver my soul from the wicked, which is thy sword:" **Psalm 17:13**
>
> "Deliver my soul from the sword; my darling from the power of the dog." **Psalm 22:20**
>
> "He hath delivered my soul in peace from the battle that was against me: for there were many with me." **Psalm 55:18**
>
> "I said, LORD, be merciful unto me: heal my soul; for I have sinned against thee." **Psalm 41:4**
>
> "But if he be found, he shall restore sevenfold (completely), he shall give all his substance of his house." **Proverbs 6:31 (amplification added)**
>
> "And I will restore to you the years that the locust hath eaten, the cankerworm, and the caterpillar, and the palmerworm, my great army which I sent among you. And ye shall eat in plenty, and be satisfied, and praise the name of the LORD your God, that hath dealt wondrously with you: and my people shall never be ashamed." **Joel 2:25-26**
>
> "Our soul is escaped as a bird out of the snare of the fowlers: the snare is broken, and we are escaped." **Psalm 124:7**
>
> "He restoreth my soul: he leadeth me in the paths of righteousness for his name's sake." **Psalm 23:3**

Get the point, yet?!! The enemy lies in wait for our souls but greater is He that's in us that he that's in the world! Praise God!

This is my prayer for you, beloved of God. I encourage you to declare it aloud as you read it:

In the name of Jesus Christ, I claim the restoration of MY soul. I break any curse and in the name of the Lord Jesus, I ask that you send as many angels as necessary to recover the parts of my mind, will, and emotions which have been fragmented by sexual sin, alcohol, drugs, unforgiveness, offense, idolatry or religious error and bring them back to place them where they belong in me. I also pray in Jesus' name that all demonic entities which were formerly substituted for the fragments of the soul be cast out now, in the name of the Lord Jesus Christ! AMEN!

DEFINITIONS

abide: vb. to stay in a given place, state, relation, to remain in a place

animate: vb. to give or fill with life; to impart interest or zest to; to enliven or make lively; to give the quality or condition of being alive, active or vigorous; to fill with spirit, courage or resolution; to inspire to action; to impart motion or activity to; to cause to possess life

apostasy: n. the abandonment or renunciation of a religious or political belief

apostate: n. one who abandons or renounces a religious or political belief

astral projection: n. the ability of a person to intentionally project their spirit to travel to distant places of their own will (outside of God's will) a variety of ethical theory and practice that emphasizes reason, scientific inquiry, and human fulfillment in the natural world and often rejects the importance of belief in God; a system of thought that rejects religious beliefs and centers on humans and our values, capacities, and worth

authority (from the Greek word *exousaizo*): vb. to have power, use power, exercise authority upon; ability or strength with which one is endued, which either possesses or exercises; to command such that one must be submitted to by others and obeyed; to enforce laws, exact obedience, command, determine, or judge

Baal: n. Canaanite god of storms, rivers and water; some text uses Hadad, a god of thunderstorms: also known as the weather god of Syria-Palestine.

beguile: vb. to seduce, trick, dupe

belief: n. mental acceptance of and the conviction in the truth, actuality, or validity of something

believe: vb. to accept as true or real; to have firm faith in; to have faith, confidence, or trust

bind (from the Greek word *deo*): vb. to fasten or tie as with chains, when Satan is bound he is made inoperable.

blasphemy: n. an absolute denouncing of God the Father, Son and/or Holy Ghost (the latter of which is listed as the one unforgiveable sin in Matthew 12:32)

bond (from the Hebrew word *ecar*): n. (legally) binding obligation

comprehend (from the Greek word *katalambano*): vb. to lay hold of (so as to make one's own); to obtain, attain to, to take into one's self; to seize upon, take possession of (especially of evil: overtaking one, of the last day overtaking the wicked with destruction, of a demon about to torment one; especially of Christ: by His holy power and influence laying hold of the human mind and will, in order to prompt and govern it); to detect, catch; to lay hold of with the mind; to understand, perceive, learn

confess[1] (from the Greek word *homologeo;* a compound word formed from the words *homo* and *logos*): vb. to say the same words as; based off of revelation received from the Holy Ghost stemming from the words *homo* (meaning same) and *logos* (meaning "word")

confess[2] (from the Greek word *homologeo*): vb. to admit or declare one's self guilty of what one is accused of

conjure: vb. to summon by incantation

corrupt: vb. to ruin, to decay, to spoil by any process; defile, destroy; to be marked by immorality and perversion; to ruin morally; to change the original form of a thing/person

cultivate: n. to foster the growth of; to loosen or break up the soil about (growing plants i.e. fruit)

Dagon: n. Philistine deity of fertility represented with the face and hands of a man and the tail of a fish (the name itself meaning "fish")

debauchery: n. extreme indulgence in bodily pleasures and especially sexual pleasures: behavior involving sex, drugs, alcohol, etc. that is often considered immoral

defile: vb. to make foul or unclean; to pollute, taint; debase; to make impure for ceremonial use; to make filthy or dirty

deliberate: adj. done with or marked by full consciousness of the nature and effects of one's actions; intentional; voluntary

deliver[1]: vb. to bring or transport to the proper place or recipient; distribute; to surrender (something or someone) to another; hand over; to secure (something promised or desired) as for a candidate or political party; to set free, as from misery, peril, or evil

deliver[2] (from the Hebrew word *natsal*): vb. to snatch away, whether in a good or bad sense; to defend, escape, preserve, recover, rescue; to tear oneself away

deliver[3] (from the Hebrew word *palat*): vb. to carry away safe; to slip out

deliver[4] (from the Hebrew word *padah*): vb. to sever; to release; to redeem

deliverance[1]: n. rescue from bondage or danger

deliverance[2] (from the Greek word *aphesis*): n. freedom, liberty, remission; forgiveness; a release from bondage

denounce: vb. to announce or proclaim something evil or calamitous

desolate: adj. deprived or destitute of inhabitants, deserted; solitary, lonely; forsaken or abandoned

desolation: n. a state of devastation waste or barrenness

detect: vb. to observe (as it relates to deliverance – to observe what spirits are doing to/through a person)

devil (from the Greek word *daimon*): n. an inferior deity (as in a god or goddess); an evil spirit; demon

discern: vb. to separate, make a distinction (recognize or noting of difference); (see 1 Corinthians 12:10)

disciple: n. one who is under discipline; a pupil, learner

discipline: n. training to act in accordance with rules

disputant: n. one that is engaged in a dispute; arguer

dissension[1] (from the Greek word *dichostasia*): n. division
dissension[2] (from the Greek word *stasis*) n. strife, disagreement

divination: n. the fortune telling practice of using the stars, tarot cards, tea leaves, crystal balls, horoscopes and palm reading to tell the future

doctrine (from the Greek word *didache*): n. that which is taught; instruction

emotion(s): n. a conscious mental reaction (as anger or fear) individually experienced as strong feeling usually directed toward a specific object or person and typically accompanied by physical and behavioral changes in the body

empowerment: n. a temporary and spontaneous increase of physical and spiritual or mental strength

encroach: vb. to advance beyond proper, established, or usual limits; to trespass upon property, domain, or rights of another, especially; by gradual advances; it also means to creep gradually and often

entice: vb. to beguile by something (as an action or speech) that tends to flatter or coax; to allure, to bait (as to catch by with bait)

expel: vb. to force or drive out; to discharge from or as if from a receptacle

folly: n. criminally or tragically foolish actions or conduct; evil, wickedness; lewd behavior

forgive (from the Greek word *apheimi*): vb. to send; to send forth; to give up a debt; in various applications: - cry, forgive, forsake, lay aside, leave, omit, put (send) away, remit, suffer, yield up

fortify: vb. to strengthen and secure (a place, such as a town) by forts; to give physical strength, courage, or endurance to

fragment: n. a part broken away from a whole; broken pieces; a detached, isolated or incomplete part; disconnected

giant (from the Hebrew word *nephiyl*): n. giants, the Nephilim (derivative of the Hebrew word *naphal*); Anakim of Philistia and Emims of Moab (see Deuteronomy 2:10-11)

habit: n. an act repeated so often that it becomes involuntary; there is no new decision of the mind each time the act is performed

habitation (from the Greek word *oiketerion*): n. a dwelling place; of the body as a dwelling place for the spirit

heresy (from the Greek word *hairesis*): n. dissensions arising from diversity of opinions and aims

holy (from the Greek word *hagios*): adj. sacred

immorality: n. not confirmed with accepted principles of right and wrong behavior (morals)

incantation: n. a use of spells or verbal charms (spoken or sung) as a part of a ritual of magic

indwelling: n. the permanent presence of God or a spiritual force in the heart or soul; an existence as an animating or divine inner spirit, force, or principle

infirmity: n. physical weakness; disease, frailty

integrity: n. the quality or state of being complete; the condition of being free from damage or defect

in union (with): adv. consecrated to the same end; one in mind, purpose and life; joined as in the covenant of marriage

judgment: n. an ability to make decisions or evaluations that are wise, reasonable and valid; a verdict pronounced judicially, especially a sentence or formal decree

Leviathan (from the Hebrew word *livyathan*): n. sea monster, dragon

loose (from the Greek word *lyo*): vb. to loose any person or thing tied or fastened; to loose one bound; to set free; to discharge from prison; to free from bondage or disease (one held by Satan) by restoration to health; loosing is setting the captive free

Lucifer (from the Hebrew word *heylel*) n. light-bearer; shining one, morning star

lust: n. desire (for what is forbidden), craving, longing

medium: n. a person through whom other persons try to communicate with the spirits of the dead (also known as a necromancer); possessor of a conjuring spirit with which the dead are conjured up for the purpose of inquiring about the future

mind (from the Greek word *nous*): n. the seat of reflective consciousness, comprising the facilities of perception and understanding and those of feeling, judging, determining; the intellective faculty; reason

mob: n. a group of persons bent on riotous living
naphal: vb. to fall, lie down, be cast down, fail

offence or offense (from the Greek word *skandalon*): n. a stumbling block, something against which causes a person to fall; a trap or snare causing one to fall or sin

offended: adj. outraged or insulted; suggests a deliberate cause of humiliation, hurt pride, pain or shame

power (from the Greek word *dynamis*): n. strength power, ability, power residing within a thing by virtue of its nature or which a person or thing exerts and puts forth; power whether by virtue of one's own ability and resources, or of state of mind, or through favorable circumstances, or by permission of law or custom; miraculous power: ability, might; (worker of) power, strength, mighty works; the word "dynamite" stems from this word

precept (from the Hebrew word *mitzvah*): n. commandment

pretence (or pretense): n. a claim made or implied especially: one not supported by fact

quicken (from the Greek word *zoopoeio*): vb. to restore to life

rail(ing): vb. to utter bitter complaint or vehement denunciation

rationalize: vb. to ascribe one's acts, opinions, etc. to causes that superficially seem reasonable and valid but that actually are unrelated to the true (possibly unconscious and often less creditable or agreeable) causes

renounce: vb. to give up or put aside voluntarily; to disown

reprobate (from the Greek word *adokimos*): adj. not standing the test; that which does not prove itself such as it ought; unfit for, unproved

restore: vb. to turn back, bring back, bring home again; carry back again; convert; deliver again; pull in again; recover, return (to a best or original state); regenerate; to make new

riotous: adj. participating in a riot

Satan: (from the Hebrew word *satan*): n. adversary, one who withstands

scorpion: n. metaphorically, a skeptic, one who doubts, questions or disagrees with piercing opposition

seduce: vb. to lead astray, as from duty; to corrupt; to lead or draw away, as from principles, faith, or allegiance; to win over; to attract or entice

serpent: n. metaphorically, a serpent is referred to as an artful, malicious person: one who is skillful in accomplishing a purpose, especially with cunning or craft; the malice, the desire to harm others or see others suffer is compared to the venom of a serpent (see Psalm 58:4, 140:3)

sin: n. transgression of divine law; any act regarded as a transgression: especially a willful or deliberate violation of some religious or moral principle; any regrettable action or behavior; great fault or offense

sober: adj. calm and collected in spirit; temperate (marked by moderation); dispassionate (not influenced by strong feeling, not affected by personal or emotional involvement); circumspect (careful to consider all circumstances and possible consequences)

sorcery (from the Greek word *pharmakeia* which is where the word pharmacy is derived from): n. magical arts induced through drugs, alcohol, suggestive dancing, charms or wearing ancestral/ancient makeup

soul tie: n. unholy connections resulting from every unsanctioned sexual partner a person has had outside of marriage (whereas, within marriage, this type of connection is sanctioned and holy)

spirit (from the Greek word *pneuma*): n. breath, life, spirit

spiritism: n. a belief that spirits of the dead communicate with the living usually through a medium

squatter: n. a person who settles on land or occupies property without title, right, or payment of rent

statute: n. an established law or regulation: an authoritative order or proclamation issued by an authority and having the force of law

stealth: n. secret, the act of practice of stealing

stronghold[1] (physical): n. an enclosure that is fortified with thick stonewalls; a fortress built with walls and defenses to provide protection against the enemy, usually built on a hill so attackers had to climb up to reach the fortress

stronghold[2] (spiritual) n. speculations and imaginations

stronghold[3] (from the Greek word *ochyroma*): n. reasonings, thoughts, and imaginations that precede and determine our conduct; the arguments and reasoning's by which a disputant endeavors to fortify his opinion and defend it against his opponent.

subvert: vb. to dismantle, overthrow, ravage or ravish (to seize and carry off by force) something already established; to overcome with emotions

torment: vb. to afflict with great bodily or mental suffering or pain; to weary or annoy excessively; to throw into commotion; stir up; to disturb

transgress: vb. to violate a law, command or moral code; to pass over or go beyond a limit or boundary imposed by a law or command; to violate: especially the will of God

tread: vb. to trample; to hit as if by a single blow, to smite, to strike; to walk on, over; to press beneath the feet; to subdue harshly or cruelly, crush (see Genesis 3: 14-15)

trespass: vb. an unlawful act causing injury to the person, property or rights of another, committed with force or violence; it is an overstepping of boundaries and assuming possession of another's property.

vex (from the Greek word *ochleo*): vb. to mob or torment

vigilant: adj. watchful; given to strict attention; cautious, active; heedful lest some destructive calamity suddenly overtake a person

vow (from the Hebrew word *nadar*): n. a promise

wholly (from the Greek word *holoteles*): adj. complete to the end, that is, absolutely perfect

will (from the Greek word *thelema*): n. what one wishes or has determined to be done; choice, inclination, desire, pleasure

witchcraft (**witch** stemming from the Indo-European word *weik* used for both the words religion and magic): n. from an old English term *wicce-craft*, referring to the art or skill of using supernatural forces to bend the world (or another person) to one's will; a religion (any system of beliefs, practices, and ethical values) that worships Satan and his demonic forces in order to receive magic power to influence and control the will of others; such practices work primarily through disobedience, which opens the door for intimidation, manipulation and domination

BIBLIOGRAPHY

1. Eckhart, John. *Let Us Alone*: *The Cry of Demons.* Chicago. Crusaders Ministries, 1995. Print.

2. Eckhart, John. *Prayers that Rout Demons: Prayers for Defeating Demons and Overthrowing the Powers of Darkness.* Chicago. Charisma House, 2007. Print.

3. Hammond, Frank and Ida Mae. *Pigs in the Parlor: A Practical Guide to Deliverance.* Kirkwood. Impact Christian Book, Inc., 2010. E-book.

4. Hammond, Frank and Ida Mae. *Pigs in the Parlor: A Practical Guide to Deliverance.* Kirkwood. Impact Christian Book, Inc., 2010. Print.

5. Merriam Webster's Dictionary. 2019. www.merriam-webster.com

6. Microsoft Bing Dictionary. 2019. www.bing.com

7. The American Heritage College Dictionary. 2019. www.ahdictionary.com

8. The Holy Bible. Biblica, 2019. www.blueletterbible.com

9. The Holy Bible. Bible Study Tools, 2019. www.biblestudytools.com

ABOUT THE AUTHOR

Prophet JoAnn C. Witherspoon is the Founder and Chief Executive of Jehovah Machseh ("God Our Refuge") Teaching and Training Center and the Visionary of "Strengthening the Prophets" School of the Prophets. Jehovah Machseh provides a place for the restoration of faith and hope to God's people through love, Christian education, prophetic and deliverance training. Through the prophetic and apostolic anointing on her life, she teaches and ministers both locally and nationally in the areas of deliverance, healing and prophecy.

JoAnn is a native of Chicago, IL and accepted her call into ministry in 1994. Born into African Methodism, she spent her childhood at the feet of her grandmother and pastor, the late Rev. Iceola Starling. JoAnn preached her initial sermon in 1995 and received her Itinerant Deacon (Minister) Licensure in 1996. She was later admitted into the National Association of Women in Ministry for her Missionary Certification and received additional training and certification in telephone prayer and counseling ministry through TBN Christian Television, formerly known as TV 38. JoAnn has served in ministry for over 25 years.

As an avid minister, missionary ("sent one") and educational administrator, JoAnn wholeheartedly served God and the

AME church for six years under the late Bishop Robert Thomas, Jr. as President of the Area Missionary Society, Praise and Worship Leader and Sunday School instructor. She also served as the assistant chaplain at the Salvation Army in 2000. Elder JoAnn's apostolic ministry was set in motion in 2002 at Crusaders Ministry in Chicago, IL under Apostles John Eckhart and Daryl O'Neal, where she received Lay-Ministry Certification/Licensure. In 2004 she began serving at House of Praise Family Church in Aurora, IL under Prophet Patrick McManus, where she was elevated to the office of Associate Pastor. In this assignment, as in all others, Elder JoAnn gave untiring leadership. She assisted in facilitating conferences, provided insight and direction to the Children and Youth Ministry teachers and also served as a member of the Prophetic Roundtable for the West/Northwest Chicago Suburb region. In 2007, she was ordained and confirmed in the Office of the Prophet through Christian International Ministries under the oversight of Bishop Bill Hamon through the confirmation, impartation and laying on of hands by Apostles Leon Walters and Pat McManus.

In 2011 the Lord began a new chapter in Prophet JoAnn's life as He transitioned her to the Dallas/Fort Worth area to establish a ministry. In 2018 she began to embrace her calling to the Apostleship, though the anointing has always been upon her. Prophet JoAnn now oversees Jehovah Machseh Teaching and Training Center and is committed to raising spiritual sons and daughters, and teaching God's people to hear His voice and speak what He says.

Prophet JoAnn resides in Coppell, TX and is the proud mother of three children; Armonie, Annjo and Adam, and grandmother of four; Arian, Morgan, Nathan and Marcus. She has also been active in supporting disaster relief efforts in
the Oklahoma area and served alongside Senior Pastors Daren and Denise Dabrowski of Firehouse Community Outreach (Moore, OK).

Prophet Joann's Personal Deliverance Testimony:

In April 2012, I was diagnosed with breast cancer. After I questioned the Lord as to why I would be afflicted with such a disease, He led me to the story of Job. In the first couple books of Job, it says that there was a day when the sons of God came to present themselves before the Lord, and Satan (the Adversary) came also among them. The story goes on to say that there was conversation that took place between God and Satan (who was searching the earth for his next victim, presumably) where the Lord asked Satan:

> *"Hast thou considered my servant Job, that there is none like him in the earth, a perfect and an upright man, one that feareth God, and escheweth evil? and still he holdeth fast his integrity, although thou movedst me against him, to destroy him (Job) without cause."* **Job 2:3 (amplification added)**

God gave permission to Satan to set forth his hand to Job but told him that he could not take his life. Well, in May 2013... I become Job. After thirty-two rounds of chemotherapy, surgery and more than thirty doses of radiation, that battle was won! So, I thought.

In November of 2013 I began to feel pain like I hadn't experienced before. Although I had suffered lower back pain for years, this pain was much worse and became more and more unbearable. For years, I had prayed and sought the Lord for my healing to which He assured me I was healed. I received many prophetic words about my healing and I believed them all. Yet, by January of 2014, it was so bad that I couldn't stand for any period of time or walk any distance without being in tears. In April 2014, I began a six-week teaching on deliverance. It was at this time that I called for every prayer warrior I knew to cover me because now the physical pain I was experiencing was becoming debilitating. I had difficulty getting dressed and I would often find myself on my knees or laid out on the floor in excruciating pain shooting from my lower back up to my left side and further up into my neck.

Finally, one Friday night I called for two of my students to pray with me concerning this attack on my body. I continued to stand on the word that I had received concerning my complete healing. I reminded God of Luke 13:16:

> *"Ought I being a daughter of Abraham, whom Satan hath bound, lo, be loosed from this bond on the Sabbath day?"*

While we were in prayer, I heard the Lord say, "Charge Michael to lead my army to annihilate your enemy." I followed them promptly upon hearing the instructions. The next morning, one of my students came to me and showed me a video on YouTube called, "No Man Can Resist My Body." What happened next was answer to prayer!!

As I watched this video I, too, began to realize how (for years before my salvation) I had used my body to commit sexual sin and debauchery. I immediately began to pray the prayers against the Leviathan and Marine Spirits that are published in
Apostle John Eckhart's book: Prayers that Rout Demons.

I called out the snake marine spirit. The next thing I heard was a loud, deep, empty and violently angry voice! It yelled: "Noooo! You belong to me!" I responded: "No, I don't! I belong to the Lord Jesus because He's my Lord and Saviour! As a matter of fact, if you didn't hear me before 22 years ago, hear me now: I renounce and denounce you! I loose myself from you and command you to come out of me now, in Jesus' name!" At that very moment, I began to regurgitate. Afterwards, I felt no pain in my lower back for the first time in years! I also noticed that much of the anger I had been fighting to keep at bay was gone. I went through the rest of the morning praising the Lord as He continued revealing to me the devil's work.

God told me that pharmakeia (witchcraft) helped hide the work of the devil and what he was doing to bring about my destruction. As long as my mind was under its spell, I couldn't focus on what was being done to my spine (spiritual blindness). Going back to the days of chemotherapy, I realize I had been exposed to this particular work. Drugs, whether legal or illegal, are designed to paralyze and steal one's personality and character. In short, they alter the mind which impacts the soul.

The devil's plan was to put me in a wheelchair from early on in my life. As a tween (between 11 and 13), I admired and even wanted to be like bow-legged people. I didn't want to be knock-kneed – this wasn't attractive. So, to force my legs to be bowed, I began to stand with my feet together as I forced my legs out and apart. Eventually, I could feel the effect it was beginning to have on my hips as I was forcing them to rotate out. In my mind, I was going to look good when I walked and I wanted people to notice. The way I see it now in hindsight, this was the devil's way of conditioning me and my body to bring souls into his kingdom. Anyone who knew me, knew me by my walk. So though there was no medical explanation, I surely had one. I worked with chiropractors for years and understood the condition of what is called subluxation and scoliosis; I had seen pictures of it. Scoliosis is a curvature of the spine that has no medical explanation. The Lord then told me to look up scoliosis. When I did, I saw it with my spiritual eyes and it brought me to tears. Then I heard this: "The devil wanted you to look like him except standing in an upright position." This reminded me of Genesis 3:14:

> *"And the LORD God said unto the serpent, Because thou hast done this, thou art cursed above all cattle, and above every beast of the field; upon thy belly shalt thou go, and dust shalt thou eat all the days of thy life:"*

The Lord told me I defeated Satan by maintaining my integrity through my cancer fight. Since I would not curse my God and die, after Satan was defeated, he sent the snake and the spirit of paralysis to finish me off. I had betrayed the devil when I repented of sexual sin years ago and he was getting even (I remember the day when the twisting began in my back). The word of the Lord says when the enemy shall come in like a flood; the Spirit of the LORD shall lift up a standard against him (see Isiah 59:19). HALLELUJAH!! The Lord has lifted a standard!

It's not finished… The Lord told me that when the devil is cast out, he leaves a path of destruction. Now, my prayer has been that this destruction (see Abaddon in Revelation 9:11) is revealed and cast out. It has been revealed: Osteoarthritis Degeneration is his name. Stay tuned… More victory is sure to come!

Made in the USA
Columbia, SC
17 October 2020